Pupil Book 6C

Series Editor: Peter Clarke

Authors: Elizabeth Jurgensen, Jeanette Mumford, Sandra Roberts, Linda Glithro

Contents

Unit 9
Page number

Week 1: Number – Addition, subtraction, multiplication and division
- Lesson 1: Mental addition and subtraction — 4
- Lesson 2: Missing numbers — 6
- Lesson 3: Order of operations (2) — 8
- Lesson 4: Marco's Cafés — 10

Week 2: Algebra
- Lesson 1: Formulae and number sequences — 12
- Lesson 2: Algebra problems — 14
- Lesson 3: Linear equations — 16
- Lesson 4: Alternative solutions — 18

Week 3: Geometry – Properties of shapes
- Lesson 1: Drawing and naming circles — 20
- Lesson 2: Circle patterns (1) — 22
- Lesson 3: Circle patterns (2) — 24
- Lesson 4: Connecting midpoints — 26

Unit 10

Week 1: Number – Multiplication and division Incl. Decimals
- Lesson 1: Multiplying decimals by a 2-digit number using the grid method — 28
- Lesson 2: Multiplying decimals by a 2-digit number using the expanded written method — 30
- Lesson 3: Multiplying decimals by a 2-digit number using the formal written method — 32
- Lesson 4: Solving word problems (4) — 34

Week 2: Number – Fractions
- Lesson 1: Fractions, factors and multiples (2) — 36
- Lesson 2: Adding and subtracting fractions (2) — 38
- Lesson 3: Fraction multiplication problems — 40
- Lesson 4: Fraction division problems — 42

Week 3: Measurement (volume and capacity)
- Lesson 1: Converting units of capacity — 44
- Lesson 2: Maritime problems — 46
- Lesson 3: Volume of cubes and cuboids — 48
- Lesson 4: Calculating volume and finding missing lengths — 50

Unit 11

Page number

Week 1: Number – Addition, subtraction, multiplication and division

Lesson 1:	BODMAS	52
Lesson 2:	BODMAS challenge	54
Lesson 3:	Number puzzles	56
Lesson 4:	Curious questions	58

Week 2: Ratio and proportion

Lesson 1:	Flora and fauna proportion problems	60
Lesson 2:	Scale factor and ratio problems	62
Lesson 3:	Building and jewellery ratios	64
Lesson 4:	Tasty ratio and proportion problems	66

Week 3: Geometry – Position and direction

Lesson 1:	Using coordinates to locate shapes (2)	68
Lesson 2:	Plotting shapes in the four quadrants (2)	70
Lesson 3:	Using coordinates to translate shapes (2)	72
Lesson 4:	Four quadrants reflection	74

Unit 12

Week 1: Number – Multiplication and division Incl. Decimals

Lesson 1:	Using divisibility tests	76
Lesson 2:	Review multiplication and division of whole numbers	78
Lesson 3:	Review multiplication and division of decimal numbers	80
Lesson 4:	Solving word problems (5)	82

Week 2: Number – Fractions (including decimals and percentages)

Lesson 1:	Percentages and prices	84
Lesson 2:	Fractions, decimals and percentages (2)	86
Lesson 3:	Fraction and decimal equivalents (3)	88
Lesson 4:	Find the fractions	90

Week 3: Statistics

Lesson 1:	Motorway café pie charts	92
Lesson 2:	Export problems	94
Lesson 3:	Carrying out a survey	96
Lesson 4:	Mainly means	98

Maths facts   100

Unit 9, Week 1, Lesson 1

Mental addition and subtraction

Perform mental calculations including large numbers

Challenge 1

1. Work out these calculations mentally.

   a. 186 430 + 40 000
   b. 271 538 − 4200
   c. 372 300 − 600
   d. 521 642 + 300 000
   e. 762 518 + 7000
   f. 487 286 − 11 000
   g. 629 360 + 800
   h. 400 763 − 12 000
   i. 840 229 − 500 000
   j. 377 224 + 8500

2. Adding or subtracting a multiple of 10, 100 or even 1000 is not difficult. What types of addition and subtraction calculations do you find difficult to calculate mentally and need to use a formal written method for? Include in your explanation some examples of these types of calculations.

Challenges 2, 3

1. Work out these calculations mentally.

   a. 2 670 000
      i. + 500 000
      ii. + 7000
      iii. − 34 000
      iv. − 300 000

   b. 4 350 800
      i. + 54 000
      ii. + 6000
      iii. − 400 000
      iv. − 3000

   c. 5 714 000
      i. + 700 000
      ii. + 8000
      iii. − 5000
      iv. − 400

d 3 157 800	e 7 000 000	f 4 390 822
i + 900	i + 175 000	i + 500
ii + 63 000	ii + 38 000	ii + 600 000
iii – 38 000	iii – 23 000	iii – 56 000
iv – 400 000	iv – 300	iv – 700 000

2 Play these two games with a partner.

More than 1 000 000

- Both write down the number 10 000. This is your start number.
- Take turns to spin the spinner and roll the dice.
- Each time, put the two together to make a number. So, if you roll a 2 and spin 'ten thousands', then your number would be 20 000.
- Add your number to the start number.
- Continue until one player's number is greater than 1 000 000. This player is the winner.

Less than 10 000

- Begin with a start number of 1 000 000.
- Play the game as described above, but this time subtract the number you make using the dice and the spinner.
- The winner is the first player whose number is less than 10 000.

You will need:
- Resource 78: Place value spinner
- pencil and paper clip – for the spinner
- 1–6 dice

Challenge 3

Develop a different version of the games in Challenges 2,3 that involves addition and subtraction.

- What will the target number be?
- What will the start number be?
- What kind of dice will you use?
- Will you want a different type of spinner?

I am going to include an unlucky number. If you roll it you miss a turn!

Unit 9, Week 1, Lesson 2

Missing numbers

- Add and subtract whole numbers and decimals using the formal written methods of columnar addition and subtraction
- Estimate and check the answer to a calculation

1 Find the missing numbers in these calculations.

a) 487 273
  + _____
   829 570

b) 328 446
  + _____
   515 228

c) 732 237
  + _____
   916 829

d) 236 472
  + _____
   851 543

e) 825 656
  + _____
  1 556 983

f) 543 864
  − _____
   328 547

g) 473 965
  − _____
   256 462

h) 726 834
  − _____
   408 519

i) 943 829
  − _____
   429 316

2 Explain how you worked out the missing numbers in Question 1.

1 Use rounding to estimate the missing numbers in each calculation. Then find the missing numbers.

a) 5 683 145
  + _____
  7 995 927

b) 4 293 562
  + _____
  6 836 296

c) _____
  + 4 382 175
  9 547 969

d) _____
  + 7 372 145
  10 853 817

e) 5 287 931
  − _____
  2 636 461

f) 7 862 975
  − _____
  4 447 492

g) 8 428 715
  − _____
  2 709 084

h) _____
  − 2 653 425
  3 719 226

i) _____
  − 2 315 463
  6 112 192

2 Find the missing decimal numbers in these calculations.

a) 56 781·23
   +   ·
   ─────────
     83 938·16

b) 48 765·41
   +   ·
   ─────────
     84 677·80

c)   ·
   + 59 232·81
   ─────────
     91 389·03

d) 87 241·34
   −   ·
   ─────────
     61 630·82

e) 94 781·59
   −   ·
   ─────────
     41 328·38

f)   ·
   − 44 256·82
   ─────────
     31 272·94

Challenge 3

1 Find three different answers for each calculation.

a) 6 2 1 7 8 5 9
   +_____
          9   3 4

b) 4 0 8 7 2 9 4
   +_____
         6   2 1

c) 5 4 8 6 7 2 1
   +_____
        9   6 9

d) 8 4 3 1 5 7 6
   −_____
        3 2   7

e) 5 2 9 4 7 6 0
   −_____
      1 3   5

f) 6 7 8 1 4 2 5
   −_____
         4 3 6

2 Check your answers to Question 1 with a partner. Do you have any of the same missing digits?

3 Work out where the missing puzzle pieces go in this addition calculation. Some pieces have been put in for you.

Hint
There are multiple solutions to this problem. See if you can find more than one.

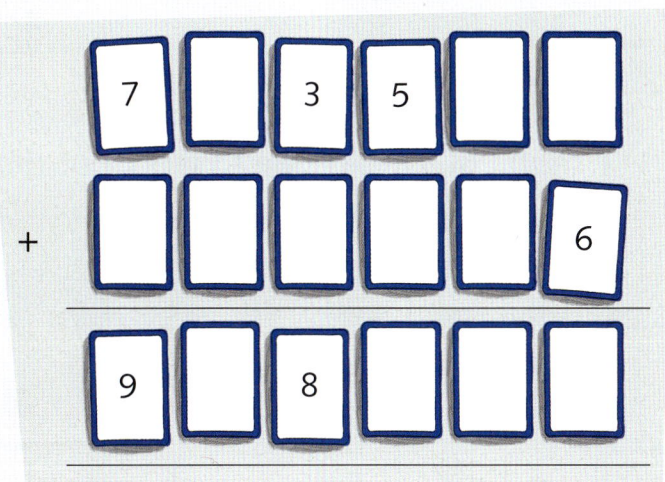

Unit 9, Week 1, Lesson 3

Order of operations (2)

Use knowledge of the order of operations to carry out calculations involving the four operations

For each calculation, estimate the answer before you work it out. Then compare your actual answer with your estimate to check your working.

Challenge 1

1 Use the BODMAS rule to work out the answers to these calculations.

a 45 + 16 × 2
b 25 + 32 ÷ 4
c 40 − 30 ÷ 5
d 32 − (5 + 7)
e 22 ÷ (15 − 4)
f 30 × (8 + 12)

Rule

BODMAS
The order for operations is:
B   Brackets
O   Orders (e.g. 4^2)
DM Division and Multiplication
AS Addition and Subtraction
The way to remember this is:
BODMAS

2 Work out each pair of calculations to see the effect of using brackets.

a (14 − 3) + 2
   14 − (3 + 2)

b (4 + 8) × 5
   4 + (8 × 5)

c (25 − 4) × 6
   25 − (4 × 6)

d (24 + 16) ÷ 8
   24 + (16 ÷ 8)

e (75 − 15) ÷ 5
   75 − (15 ÷ 5)

f (36 ÷ 6) + 3
   36 ÷ (6 + 3)

Challenge 2

1 Use the BODMAS rule to work out the answers to these calculations.

a 297 ÷ 9 × 3 + 450
b 22 × (3 + 5) − 42
c 302 + (48 − 23) × 5
d 250 + 3 × (8 + 4)
e 350 − (57 + 23) ÷ 10
f 23 × 6 − (123 − 94)
g 95 ÷ 5 − (99 − 83)
h 909 − (823 − 21) + 99
i 285 ÷ 3 − (98 − 23)
j 62 + 15 × 5 ÷ 3
k 856 − (232 + 68) ÷ 10
l 200 − (36 + 27) × 2

8

2 Using the numbers and the operations below, with either one or two sets of brackets, make ten calculations. Each calculation must have a different answer and use three operations.

Challenge 3

1 Use brackets to make two different answers for each calculation: the lowest possible answer and the highest possible answer.

> **Example**
> 58 + 60 ÷ 10 − 4
> lowest answer: (58 + 60) ÷ 10 − 4 = 7·8
> highest answer: 58 + 60 ÷ (10 − 4) = 68

a 422 − 239 + 52 − 50   b 25 + 30 × 2 + 38

c 64 + 25 × 15 − 7   d 216 − 9 × 8 − 5

e 112 + 56 ÷ 7 + 14   f 95 + 190 ÷ 10 + 9

g 243 + 27 ÷ 9 − 3   h 936 − 429 ÷ 13 − 2

i 51 × 9 − 6 + 53   j 35 × 6 − 18 + 2

k 840 ÷ 5 + 3 × 25   l 53 × 3 + 42 − 98

m 144 ÷ 8 × 4 + 16

Hint
Remember, brackets can go round more than two numbers and one operation.

2 Write five calculations, each with three operations, where the answer is the same no matter where you put the brackets. Explain why this is.

Unit 9, Week 1, Lesson 4

Marco's Cafés

Solve problems involving addition, subtraction, multiplication and division

For each of these these word problems about Marco's Cafés, use rounding or the inverse operation(s) to check your answers.

Challenge 1

1. In December, Marco's customers each paid an extra 5c for a cup of coffee. This additional charge was donated to a local charity. If Marco sold 3765 cups of coffee, how much did the charity receive?

2. The café's speciality is fresh donuts. They are very popular! In November: Café P sold 5472, Café Q sold double this number, and Café R sold 4928. What were the total sales?

3. Marco ordered new cutlery for his cafés. In total he ordered 45 870 items. He ordered 20 450 teaspoons, as they are always getting lost, and an equal number of knives and forks. How many knives were ordered?

4. Marco wants new tables for his cafés. The number he needs can be:
   - divided by 3 with a remainder of 1
   - divided by 5 with a remainder of 3
   - divided by 6 with a remainder of 4.

   He needs between 50 and 60 tables. How many tables does he need?

Challenge 2

1. Marco orders his annual stock of napkins for all three of his cafés at the same time. Café R needs more napkins than Café Q, but not as many as Café P. One café needs 48 680 napkins and another café needs 5240 more. In total he orders 154 340 napkins. How many does he need to deliver to each café?

2. Marco checked the number of customers who have visited all three cafés. The total for February was 2311. In March the figure was five times as many. April was also a very busy month. The number of customers for all three months was 28 756. How many visited the cafés each month?

3. Every December Marco's customers pay an extra 3c for each fruit pie they buy. This additional charge is donated to charity. Last year, €125·40 was raised. This year an extra 20% was raised. How many fruit pies were sold this year and last year?

4. In January, Marco was very surprised when he looked at the donut sales in each café. He noticed that they were three consecutive numbers. The total sales were 13 665. What were the sales for each café?

5. Marco pays his staff €8 an hour. In three weeks one employee earned €888. Each week he worked 6 hours more than the week before. How many hours did he work each week?

Challenge 3

1. For August, September and October, Marco decided to order cups and paper towels and share them equally between all three of his cafés. The combined total of cups and paper towels he ordered was 25 890. He ordered 3942 more paper towels than cups.

   a How many paper towels will each café receive?

   b How many cups will each café receive?

2. In June, Marco's customers each pay an extra 5c for every cup of tea they buy. This additional charge is donated to charity. The three cafés together raised €347·60.

   a How many cups of tea were sold?

   b Café P raised 10% more than Café Q. Café R raised €81·95. How much did Cafés P and Q each raise?

Unit 9, Week 2, Lesson 1

Formulae and number sequences

- Use simple formulae
- Generate and describe linear number sequences

Challenge 1

1 Simplify expressions **a** to **d** and multiply the brackets in expressions **e** to **h**.

  a $3a + 4a + a$
  b $4x + 3y - y + 2x$
  c $5m - 3n + m - 2n$
  d $5s + 5t - 3t + 3s$
  e $2(a + b)$
  f $5(2x - y)$
  g $3(m + 3n)$
  h $4(2s - 3t)$

2 Calculate the next five numbers in these sequences and explain the rule.

  a 6, 10, 14, 18, , , ,
  b 80, 72, 64, 56, , , ,

Challenge 2

1 Simplify these expressions by grouping like terms and multiplying the brackets.

  a $4(a + 4a + b - 3b)$
  b $2(2x + 3y - y + 4x)$
  c $3(m + 2n + 2m - 4n)$
  d $3(2s + 4t - t + 2s)$
  e $5(3m + 4n - 2m - n)$
  f $4(3x - 2y - 2x + 3y)$

2 Look at these problems and decide which of the equations gives the correct solution. There may be one or two correct solutions.

  a Sam had 23 coins in his pocket and used some to buy an ice-cream. He had 11 coins left in his pocket. How many did he use?

  $11x = 23$ $11 + x = 23$ $23 + 11 = x$ $23 - x = 11$

  b Steve bought a number of pizzas and cut each one into 8 pieces. He had 56 pieces. How many pizzas did he buy?

  $p = 56 - 8$ $8p = 56$ $56p = 8$ $p = 56 \times 8$

c The school netball team played 8 matches against other schools and scored 32 goals. What is the equation to show the average number of goals scored?

   $g = 8 \div 32$ $g = 32 \div 8$
   $8g = 32$ $32g = 8$

d A rower trains on his rowing machine by rowing 15 km every day except Sunday. How far does he row each week?

   $d = 15 \times 7$ $d = 15 + 6$
   $d = 15 \div 6$ $d = 15 \times 6$

3 The nth term in a sequence is $2n - 4$. Calculate the first five terms, the 10th term and the 200th term.

4 The nth term in a sequence is $3n + 7$. Calculate the first five terms, the 10th term and the 200th term.

Challenge 3

1 Simplify these expressions by multiplying the brackets and grouping like terms.

   a $2(3x + y) + 3(2y - x)$ b $6(3a - 2a) + 8(2b - b)$
   c $3(2x - y) + 2(x + 3y)$ d $4(2a + 2b) + 2(3a - 3b)$
   e $4(t + 5s) + 3(2t - 4s)$ f $5(2a + 2b - a - b) + 4(b - a)$

2 Calculate the next five numbers in these sequences. Work out the nth term and calculate a value for the 100th term and the 250th term.

   a 6, 10, 14, , , , , n^{th} term   100th term   250th term
   b 3, 10, 17, , , , , n^{th} term   100th term   250th term

Unit 9, Week 2, Lesson 2

Algebra problems

- Express missing number problems algebraically
- Use simple formulae

Challenge 1

Four boys are throwing javelins.

- Tom threw a javelin x metres.
- John threw a javelin half as far as Tom.
- Jim threw a javelin 12 metres further than John.
- Jack's throw was 3 metres less than Tom.

a Write expressions using x for how far John, Jim and Jack threw their javelins.

b If $x = 50$ m, calculate how far each of the boys threw the javelin.

Challenge 2

1 Find the value of x.

   a $3x = 2x + 3$ **b** $2x - 4 = x + 3$ **c** $2 + 3x = x + 4$ **d** $6x - 20 = 10 + x$

2 Three families visit a Theme Park. 'c' is the cost of admission for a child and 'a' is the cost of admission to the Theme Park for an adult. Write an expression for the entry cost for each family.

   a Andrews family   **b** Barnes family   **c** Singh family

3 If the cost for a child is €12 and the cost for an adult is €21, calculate the cost for each family and then for your own family.

4 These are the five Platonic solids. They are very special because every face is a regular polygon of the same size and shape: that's why we use them as dice.

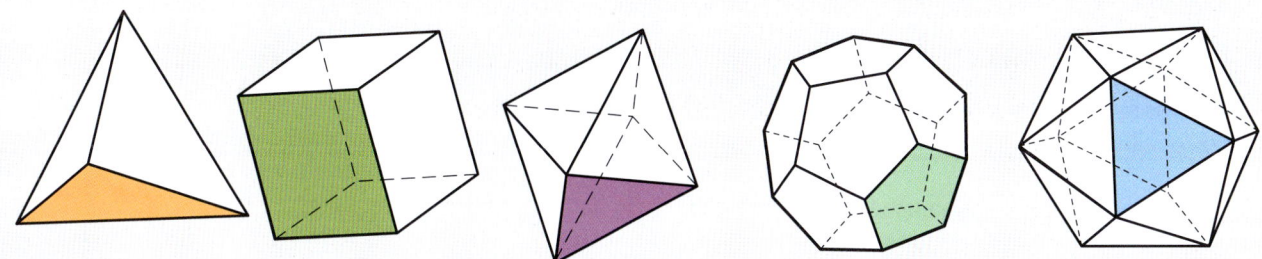

a Draw a table showing the number of faces (F), vertices (V) and edges (E) for the 5 Platonic solids. Add an extra column for 'F + V'.

b Use the information from the table to write an equation relating F, V and E.

c Do the triangular prism and hexagonal pyramid shown below fit the formula? Choose two more 3-D shapes and see if they fit the formula.

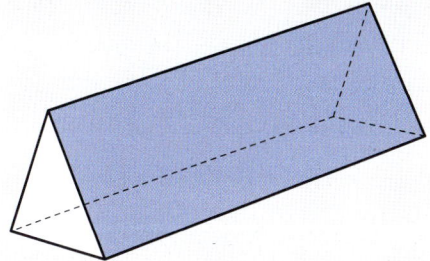 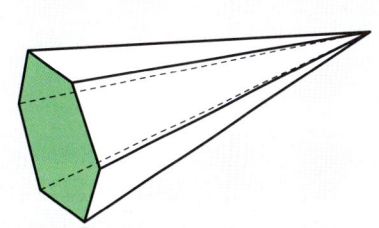

Challenge 3

There are three commonly used temperature scales:

- In Europe, the Celsius scale (°C) is generally used.
- In America, the Fahrenheit scale (°F) is generally used.
- Scientists all over the world use the Kelvin scale (K).

Copy the table below and use the formulas in the Rule box to fill in the missing temperatures.

°Fahrenheit	°Celsius	Kelvin
	0°	
140°		
	37°	
212°		

Rule

- To convert from °Fahrenheit to °Celsius: $C = \frac{5}{9}(F - 32)$
- To convert from °Celsius to °Fahrenheit: $F = \frac{9}{5}C + 32$
- To convert from °Celsius to Kelvin: $K = C + 273$

Unit 9, Week 2, Lesson 3

Linear equations

- Find pairs of numbers that satisfy an equation with two unknowns
- Use simple formulae

Challenge 1

1 Here are some sets of coordinate pairs. Complete the rules.

You will need:
- 1 cm squared graph paper
- ruler

Example
(1, 3); (2, 4); (4, 6); (7, 9)   The rule is $y = x + 2$

a (2, 5); (4, 7); (5, 8); (6, 9)   The rule is $y = x +$

b (2, 7); (3, 8); (4, 9); (6, 11)   The rule is $y = x +$

c (4, 3); (7, 6); (9, 8); (10, 9)   The rule is $y = x \ldots$

2 Use your answers from Question 1 and follow the steps below.

- Draw axes on your graph paper and label the x- and y-axes from 0 to 12.
- Plot the points from Question 1 and carefully join the coordinates to show lines **a**, **b** and **c**. Label each line.
- Write what you notice about the lines.

3 There is more than one whole number solution for each of these equations. Find two pairs of numbers that satisfy each equation.

a $2x + y = 8$ b $a + 3b = 10$

Challenge 2

1 Draw axes on your 1 cm squared graph paper and label the x- and y-axes from 0 to 15.

- Copy the table and complete the values for y.
- Plot the points and carefully join the coordinates to show the three lines. Label each line.
- Write what you notice about the lines.
- Can you draw another line that follows the same pattern? Write down the equation for your line.

	1st set of coordinates		2nd set of coordinates		3rd set of coordinates	
	x	y	x	y	x	y
$y = x + 1$	1		3		7	
$y = x + 4$	2		5		8	
$y = x + 7$	0		2		6	

16

2 There is more than one whole number solution for each of these equations. Find two pairs of numbers that satisfy each equation.

    a $a + 2b = 12$ **b** $x + 3y = 12$ **c** $2a + 3b = 16$ **d** $5x + 2y = 24$

3 Conversion graphs are commonly used to change units from one to another. Use the rules to draw separate conversion graphs for:

    a litres to pints   **b** kilograms to pounds

> **Rules**
> - 4·5 l = 8 pints
> - 5 kg = 11 lb

4 Use your graphs from Question 3 to calculate an approximate value for:

    a 6 pints in litres   **b** 3 kg in pounds

    c 7 litres in pints   **d** 15 pounds in kg

> **Hint**
> You need two points to draw a line. The second point can be (0,0).

Challenge 3

Draw axes on your 1 cm squared graph paper and label the x- and y-axes from −10 to +10 to create a 4-quadrant coordinates grid.

- Plot the line $y = x - 3$. Find values for y when $x = -5$, 2 and 6 to give you three sets of coordinates.
- Write the coordinates for the points where the line crosses the x- and y-axes.
- Now plot the line $y = x + 3$. Find values for y when $x = -6, -2$ and 4.
- Write the coordinates for the points where the line crosses the x- and y-axes. What do you notice about the two lines?
- Predict where the lines $y = x - 6$ and $y = x + 6$ will cross the x- and y-axes.
- Find three sets of coordinates for each of the lines and plot the lines to check your prediction.

Unit 9, Week 2, Lesson 4

Alternative solutions

- List possible combinations of variables
- Use simple formulae

Hint
Try to be systematic – perhaps using a table to record your results.

Challenge 1

There are 12 legs in the farmyard.

Write an equation to show the possible combinations of chickens and sheep.

Use c for the number of chickens and s for the number of sheep.

List the solutions for c and s.

Challenge 2

1 There are 28 legs in the farmyard.

Write an equation to show the possible combinations of ducks and goats.

Use d for the number of ducks and g for the number of goats.

List the solutions for d and g.

2 Here are some addition algebra 'brick wall' problems. The numbers in two bricks that are side by side are added together and make the answer in the brick above.

a How many different solutions can you find for a and b if a and b are positive integers?

b How many different solutions can you find if x and y are positive integers?

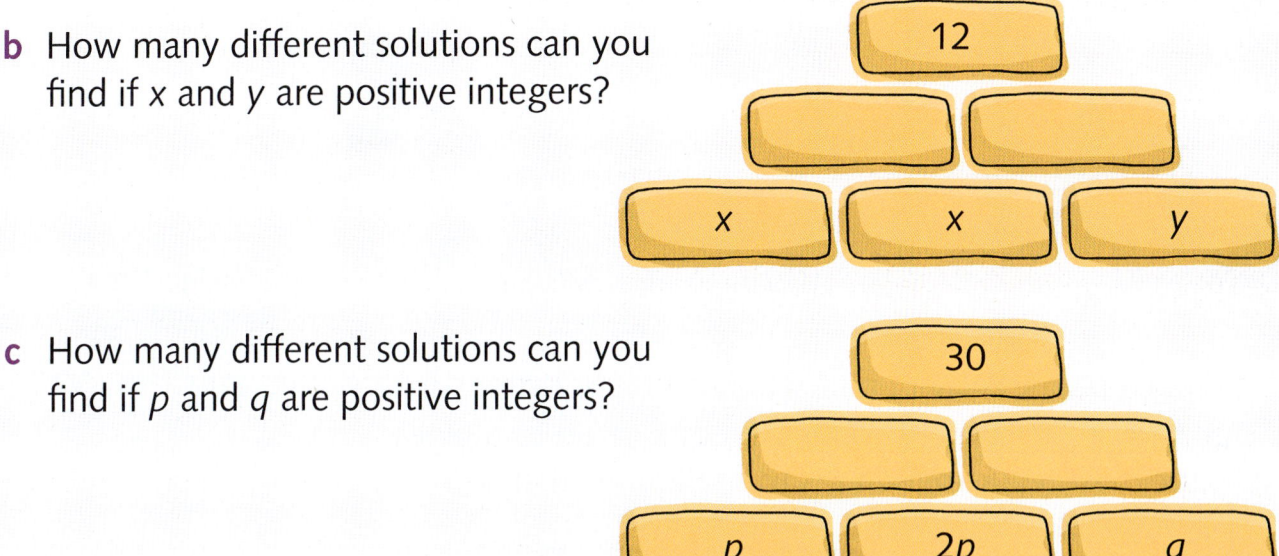

c How many different solutions can you find if p and q are positive integers?

d How can you be sure that you have found all the possible answers?

Challenge 3

1 There are 10 legs in the farmyard. Write an equation to show the possible combinations of chickens, ducks, sheep and goats. Use c for the number of chickens, d for the number of ducks, s for the number of sheep and g for the number of goats. List the solutions for c, d, s and g.

2 Here are some subtraction algebra 'brick wall' problems. The difference between the two numbers in adjacent bricks is calculated to make the answer in the brick above. Work with a partner to find three different solutions to each problem.

3 Can you and a partner find three different solutions to this multiplication algebra 'brick wall' problem?

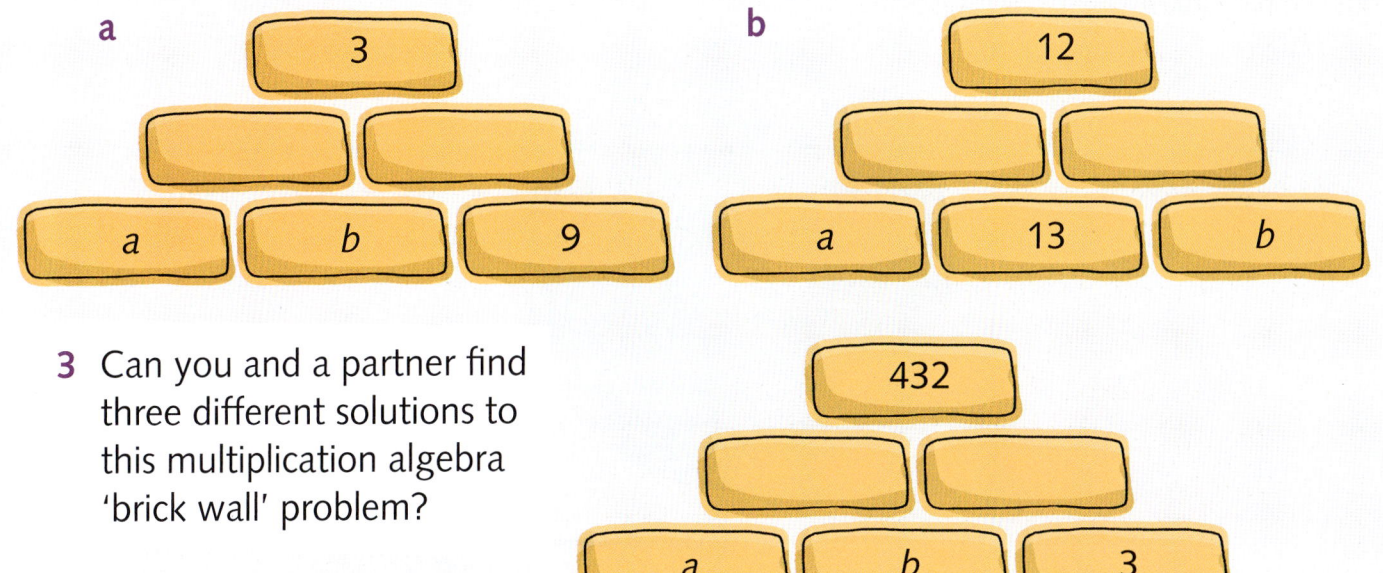

19

Unit 9, Week 3, Lesson 1

Drawing and naming circles

Draw and name parts of circles and know that the diameter is twice the radius

You will need:
- three paper circles
- glue
- ruler

 Challenges 1, 2, 3 Fold each paper circle in half. Then fold it in half again. Stick the circles into your exercise book or on to a piece of paper. Use your fold marks to mark and label each circle as shown below.

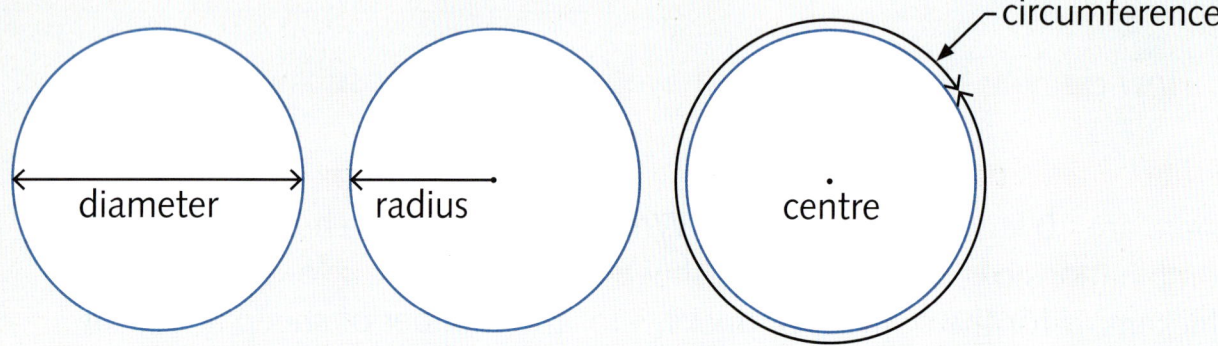

Challenge 2

1 Copy this table. Measure the diameter and the radius of each circle below and complete your table.

You will need:
- compasses
- ruler

Circle	A	B	C	D	E
Diameter (cm)					
Radius (cm)					

A

B

C

D

E

20

2. Using the rule, $d = 2r$, calculate the diameter of each circle. The circles are not drawn to scale.

Example
$r = 3.5$ cm
$d = 2 \times 3.5$ cm
$= 7$ cm

A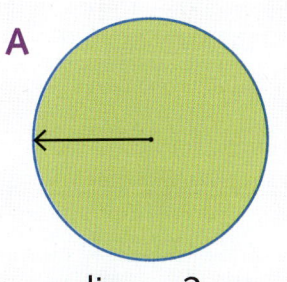
radius = 2 cm

B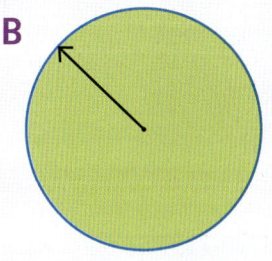
radius = 6 cm

C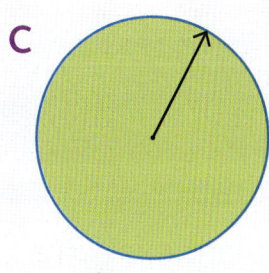
radius = 4 cm

D
radius = 2.5 cm

E
radius = 5.5 cm

F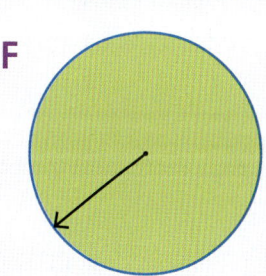
radius = 3.5 cm

3. Draw the circles in Question 2 and measure their diameters to check your calculations.

4. Using the rule, $d = 2r$, calculate the radius of each circle. The circles are not drawn to scale.

Example
$d = 9$ cm
$r = 9$ cm $\div 2$
$= 4.5$ cm

A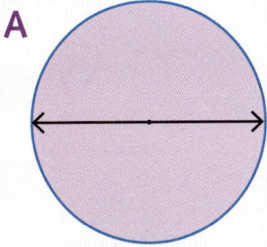
diameter = 12 cm

B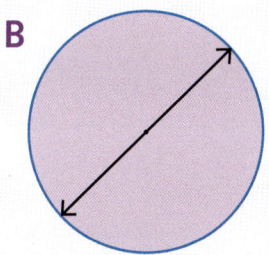
diameter = 15 cm

C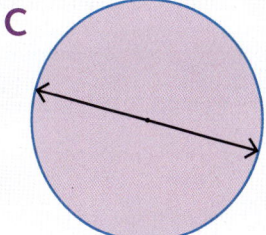
diameter = 19 cm

Challenge 3

Using the reverse side of the 1 cm squared paper and your ruler, draw eight squares with sides of 4 cm, as shown below. Set your compasses to a radius of 2 cm. Make an accurate drawing of the border pattern.

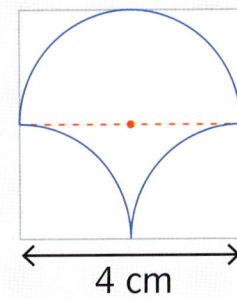
4 cm

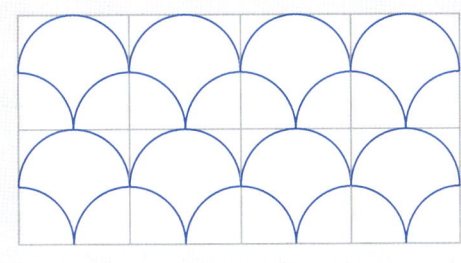

You will need:
- 1 cm squared paper
- ruler
- compasses

21

Unit 9, Week 3, Lesson 2

Circle patterns (1)

Use compasses to construct a regular hexagon and patterns based on the hexagon

1 Construct a regular hexagon using compasses.

Step 1 Set your compasses to a radius of 4 cm and draw a circle.

Step 2 With your compasses still set to a radius of 4 cm, go round the circumference of the circle, making marks 4 cm apart.

Step 3 Use your ruler to join the points where the marks cross the circle.

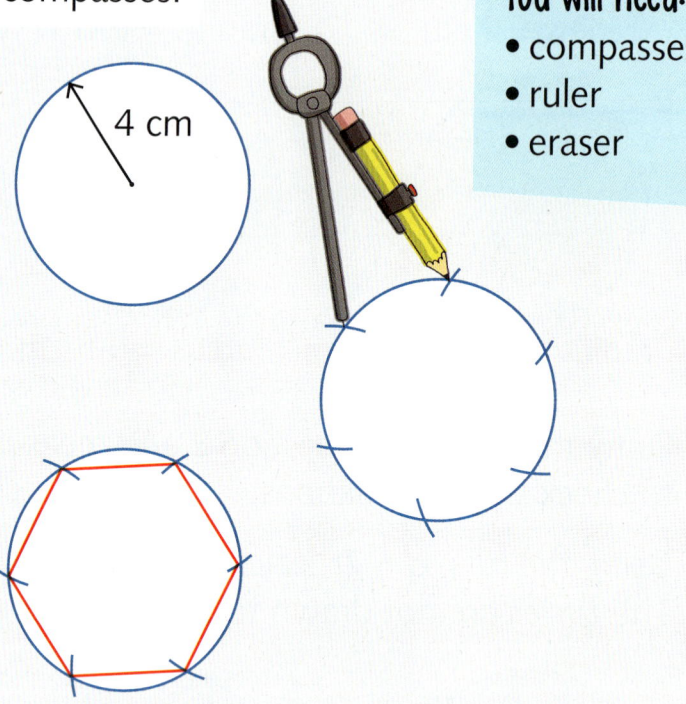

You will need:
- compasses
- ruler
- eraser

2 Using your ruler, construct six equilateral triangles within the hexagon.

1 Construct a basic hexagonal pattern using compasses.

- Follow Steps 1 and 2 in Question 1 of the Challenge above.
- Using one of the marks on the circumference as the centre, draw an arc to cut the circumference twice.
- Repeat five times more, using each mark on the circumference in turn.

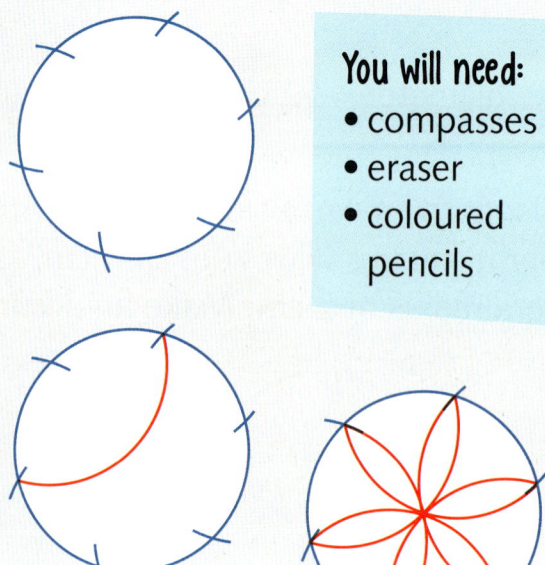

You will need:
- compasses
- eraser
- coloured pencils

2. The three designs below are based on the hexagonal pattern. Set your compasses to a radius of 3 cm. Draw each design. Erase the unwanted lines and colour the pattern.

3. Design a hexagonal pattern of your own.

Challenge 3

PQRS is a square with sides of 6 cm. Each vertex P, Q, R and S is the centre of a circle which has a radius of 4·2 cm.

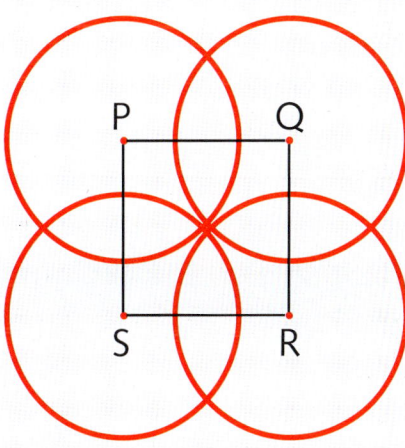

You will need:
- compasses
- protractor
- ruler
- eraser
- coloured pencils

The three designs below have been constructed using the measurements in the square pattern above. Work out how each design has been made. Choose two designs to construct and colour.

  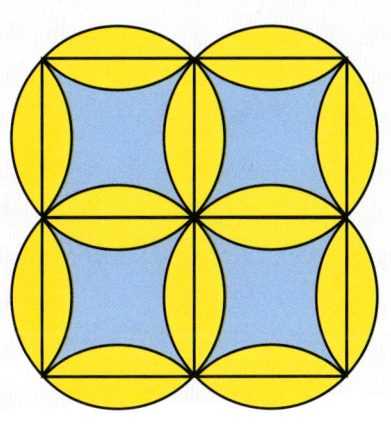

23

Unit 9, Week 3, Lesson 3

Circle patterns (2)

Use compasses to construct patterns that are based on the radius of a circle

You will need:
- card
- scissors
- ruler
- compasses
- coloured pencils

 Follow the instructions below to construct the pattern.

- Cut out a square of card with sides of 6 cm. Use your ruler to draw one of the diagonals of the square.

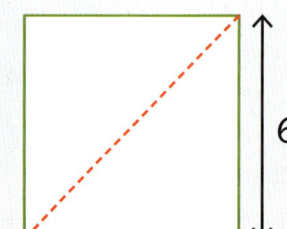

- Draw a circle with a radius of 4·2 cm in your book or on a different piece of paper. Make six marks on the circumference with your compasses set at 4·2 cm.

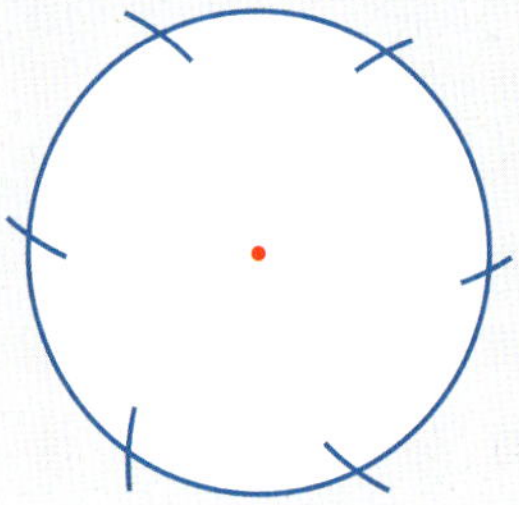

- Join the opposite marks on the circumference to make three diagonals.

- Place the square over the circle. Line up the diagonal of the square with a diagonal of the circle. Draw around the square in pencil.

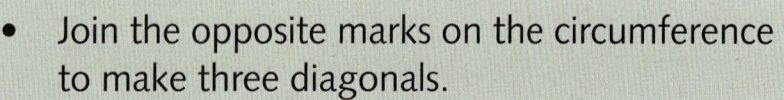

- Turn the square until it lines up with the next diagonal of the circle. Draw round the square. Repeat once more. Then colour your pattern.

24

Challenge 2

1. Draw a circle with a radius of 5 cm and construct the basic hexagonal pattern. Draw all the lines in this diagram lightly because some will be erased later.

   Then follow these steps to make your design.

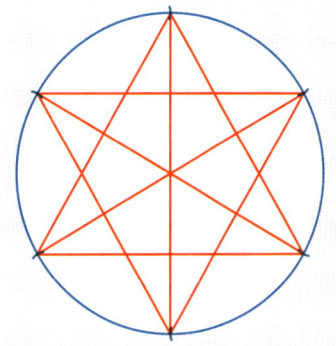

You will need:
- ruler
- compasses
- coloured pencils
- eraser

- Erase the circle.

- Repeat the hexagonal pattern.

- Then erase some lines inside the first pattern.

- Finish with one of these two designs.

- Colour your pattern to make a shape that has a sense of rotation.

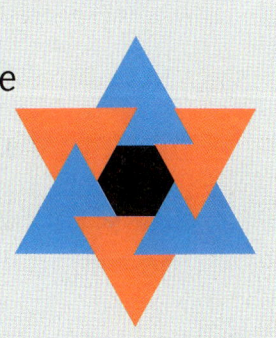

2. Start with a basic hexagonal pattern and make your own 'rotating' shape.

Challenge 3

Using the basic hexagonal pattern, construct the designs below.

You will need:
- ruler
- compasses
- coloured pencils
- eraser

Unit 9, Week 3, Lesson 4

Connecting midpoints

Draw 2-D shapes accurately and use conventional markings for lines and angles

You will need:
- Resource 63: Connecting midpoints
- ruler

 1 In triangle ABC the midpoint of each side is marked by the letters D, E and F.

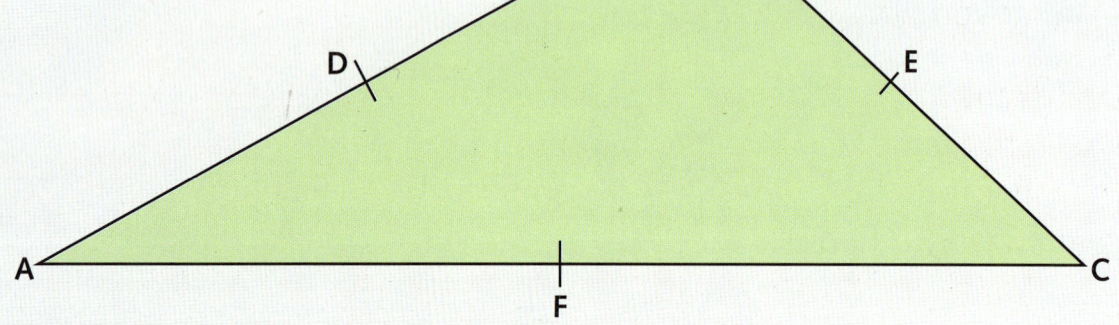

a Measure these lines to the nearest millimetre.

  i line AC   ii line AF   iii line FC

b Write the lines that are equal.

2 On Resource 63: Connecting midpoints, use your ruler to join the midpoints D and E.

a Measure the line DE to the nearest millimetre.

b Write what you notice about the lengths of the lines DE and AC.

Challenge 2

1 On Resource 63: Connecting midpoints, use your ruler to join the midpoints D and F.

You will need:
- Resource 63: Connecting midpoints
- ruler
- protractor
- 1 cm squared paper

a Measure the lines BC and DF to the nearest millimetre. Write what you notice about the two lengths.

b Measure ∠ABC, ∠ACB, ∠ADF, ∠AFD to the nearest degree. Write what you notice about the angles. Use single and double arcs to mark each pair of equal angles.

2 Draw a 12 cm by 6 cm rectangle on 1 cm squared paper.
   - Mark the midpoints of the sides of the rectangle and join them as in the diagram.
   - Mark the midpoints of the sides of the rhombus and join them as in the diagram.

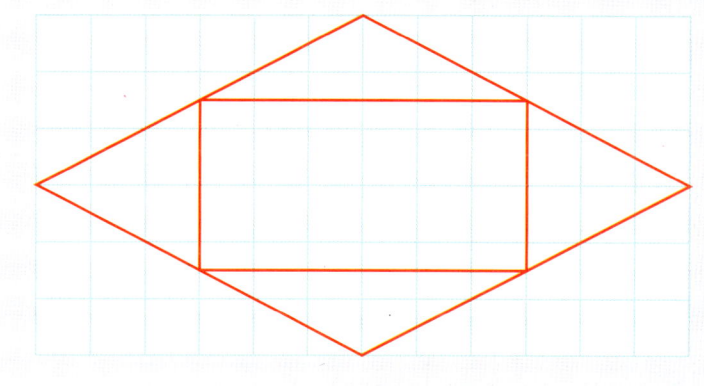

   a Measure and calculate the perimeter of the inner and outer rectangles.

   b Write what you notice about the two lengths.

3 Draw a different size rectangle on 1 cm squared paper. Join the midpoints in the same way you did in Question 2 until you have made the inner rectangle. Measure and compare the perimeters of the two rectangles you have drawn.

Challenge 3

1 On 1 cm squared paper, draw a parallelogram. Mark the midpoints of the sides of the parallelogram and join them. Then mark the mid points of the inner parallelogram and join them. Compare the perimeters of the the inner and outer parallelograms.

You will need:
- ruler
- 1 cm squared paper

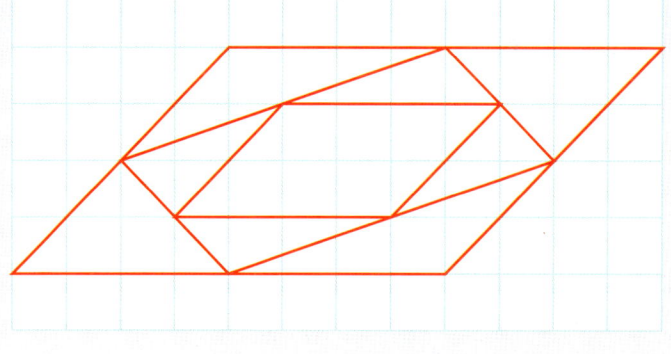

2 On 1 cm squared paper, draw an isosceles trapezium. Mark the midpoints of the sides of the trapezium and join them. Then mark the mid points of the inner shape and join them. Compare the perimeters of the inner and outer shapes.

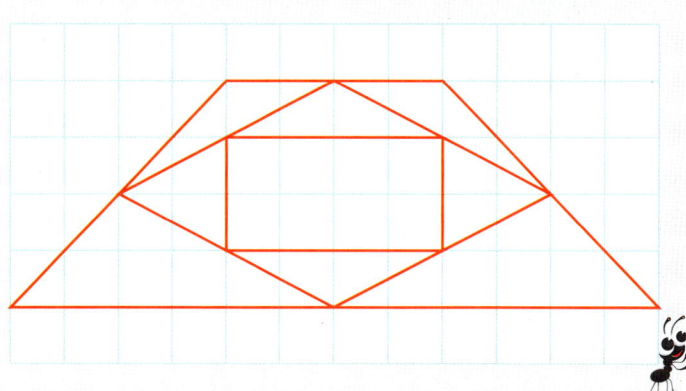

27

Unit 10, Week 1, Lesson 1

Multiplying decimals by a 2-digit number using the grid method

- Multiply a decimal by a 2-digit number using the grid method
- Estimate and check the answer to a calculation

1 For each machine, work out the output number for each input number.

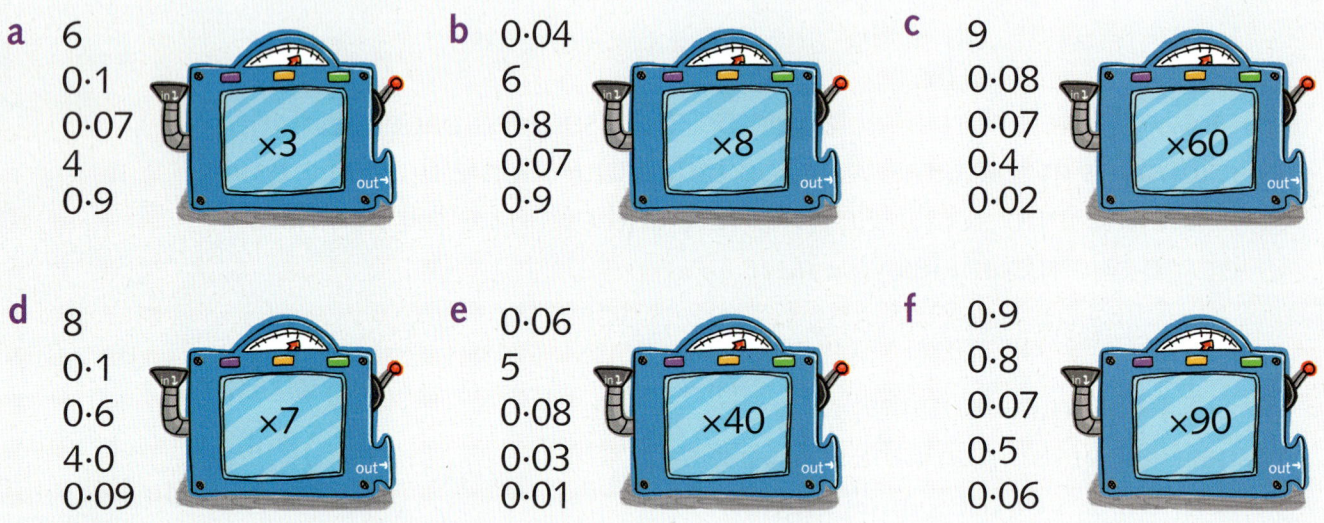

2 Find the total of the output numbers for each machine above.

3 Place the machines in order, smallest output total to largest output total.

4 Find the difference between the machine with the smallest and the machine with the largest total output.

5 Each of the machines above has been given an additional multiplication function to complete. Multiply each output answer from the sets above by the number shown below to find the new answers.

- Set **a** – multiply by 60
- Set **b** – multiply by 10
- Set **c** – multiply by 50
- Set **d** – multiply by 40
- Set **e** – multiply by 70
- Set **f** – multiply by 20

Challenge 2

Estimate the answer to each calculation. Find the answer using the grid method. Then compare your answer with your estimate.

Example

2·64 × 38 → 3 × 40 = 120

×	2	0·6	0·04
30	60	18	1·2
8	16	4·8	0·32

$$\begin{array}{r} 79·20 \\ + 21·12 \\ \hline 100·32 \\ 1 \end{array}$$

a 3·46 × 35
b 6·71 × 93
c 5·45 × 84
d 3·86 × 45
e 8·26 × 25
f 5·75 × 43
g 8·65 × 19
h 7·35 × 18
i 3·28 × 28
j 9·83 × 47
k 2·67 × 89
l 9·07 × 34
m 4·89 × 16
n 1·89 × 57
o 6·47 × 36
p 8·18 × 81

Challenge 3

Use each of the five digit cards once in each calculation in that box. Make a calculation that gives the answer shown.

Cards: 1 3 5 7 9

a ☐·☐ × ☐☐ = 75·27
b ☐·☐ × ☐☐ = 126·75
c ☐·☐ × ☐☐ = 694·45

Cards: 2 4 6 8 0

d ☐·☐ × ☐☐ = 93·60
e ☐·☐ × ☐☐ = 288·96
f ☐·☐ × ☐☐ = 36·12

Unit 10, Week 1, Lesson 2

Multiplying decimals by a 2-digit number using the expanded written method

- Multiply a decimal by a 2-digit number using the expanded written method of long multiplication
- Estimate and check the answer to a calculation

Challenge 1

What number is each clue describing?

a It is six times larger than 0·09.
b It is 0·6 more than triple 0·05.
c It is 100 times larger than 0·07 multiplied by 6.
d It is one quarter of 100.
e It is double 3·9 and double again.
f It is 10 less than when you multiply 50 by 0·5.
g It is 8 times more than 8·9.
h It is 10 times smaller than 0·5.
i It is half of 0·32 and half again.
j It is the sum of 7 multiplied by 0·07 and 0·25 multiplied by 4.
k It is the same as 2·22 multiplied by 4 add 3 multiplied by 3·33.
l It is 5 times larger than 2·3 multiplied by 2.

Challenge 2

Find the answer to these calculations using the expanded written method of long multiplication. Estimate the answer first. Convert the decimals to whole numbers, carry out the calculation, then convert the answer back to a decimal.

a 2·38 × 25
b 4·55 × 46
c 6·84 × 31
d 5·78 × 56
e 6·74 × 28
f 8·76 × 15
g 3·45 × 19
h 2·78 × 35
i 6·38 × 42
j 6·74 × 27
k 7·35 × 18
l 3·98 × 51
m 8·06 × 37
n 5·40 × 75
o 9·38 × 19

Example

5·37 × 33 → 5 × 30 = 150

		5	3	7	
	×		3	3	
		1	6¹	1²	1	(537 × 3)
	1	6¹	1²	1	0	(537 × 30)
	1	7	7	2	1

5·37 × 33 is equivalent to 537 × 33 ÷ 100.

This equals 17 721 ÷ 100, which is 177·21.

5·37 × 33 = 177·21

Challenge 3

1. Work out the total cost of each purchase. Write your answer in euros (€).

a 13 boxes of eggs costing €3.59 each.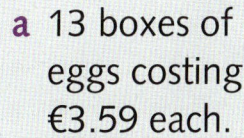

b 29 bottles of juice costing €2.89 each.

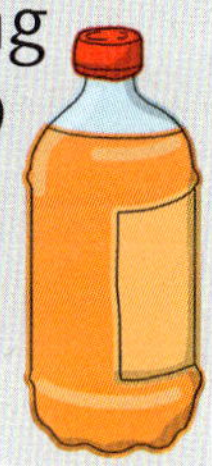

c 46 hamburgers costing €5.38 each.

d 38 pizzas costing €6.29 each.

e 54 cupcakes costing €1.96 each.

f 25 bottles of olive oil costing €4.85 each.

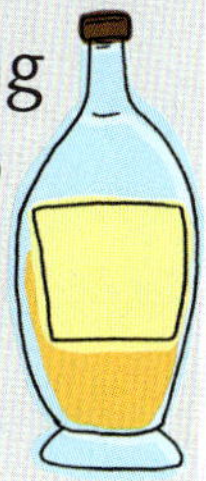

g 17 loaves of bread costing €2.49 each.

h 94 milkshakes costing €3.26 each.

i 67 pencils costing €0.79 each.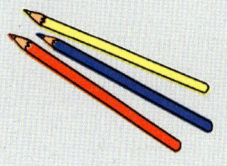

j 78 chocolate bars costing €1.95 each.

2. Work out the total cost of each purchase. Think carefully about how you are going to work out the answer: using a mental or a written method. Write your answer in euros (€).

a 18 books costing €8.55 each.

b 62 pies costing €5.90 each.

c 43 bags of popcorn costing €3.70 each.

d 39 hotdogs costing €4.80 each.

e 76 sandwiches costing €4.10 each.

f 56 cans of soup costing €1.76 each.

g 38 large cakes costing €9.39 each.

h 27 bags costing €7.39 each.

i 69 candles costing €3.67 each.

j 48 pens costing €2.89 each.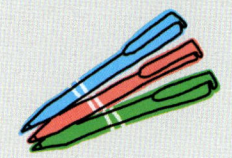

31

Unit 10, Week 1, Lesson 3

Multiplying decimals by a 2-digit number using the formal written method

- Multiply a decimal by a 2-digit number using the formal written method of long multiplication
- Estimate and check the answer to a calculation

Challenge 1

1 Work out these calculations.

a	b	c	d
600 × 9	70 × 50	800 × 6	70 × 70
60 × 90	700 × 5	80 × 6	700 × 7
60 × 9	70 × 5	80 × 6	70 × 7
6 × 9	7 × 5	80 × 60	7 × 7
0·6 × 9	0·7 × 5	0·8 × 6	7 × 0·7
0·06 × 9	0·07 × 5	0·08 × 6	7 × 0·07

e	f	g
30 × 90	110 × 40	1200 × 7
300 × 9	1100 × 4	120 × 70
30 × 9	110 × 4	120 × 7
3 × 9	11 × 4	12 × 7
0·3 × 9	11 × 0·4	12 × 0·7
0·03 × 9	11 × 0·04	0·12 × 7

2 Write five multiplication calculations that give a total of each of the numbers below.

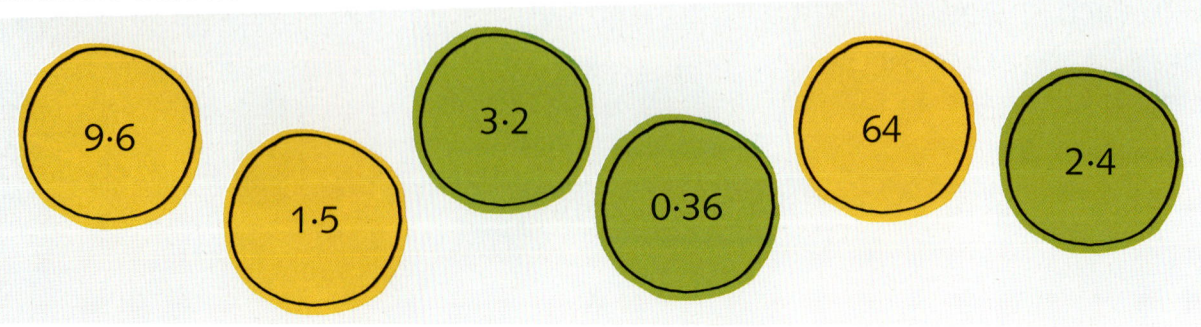

9·6   1·5   3·2   0·36   64   2·4

Challenge 2

Find the answer to these calculations using the formal written method of long multiplication. Estimate the answer first. Convert the decimals to whole numbers, carry out the calculation, then convert the answer back to a decimal.

a 6·34 × 18
b 4·73 × 34
c 7·93 × 29
d 2·78 × 75
e 7·54 × 26
f 8·94 × 63
g 7·25 × 14
h 8·29 × 25
i 9·86 × 37
j 6·42 × 58

Example

2·46 × 38 → 2 × 40 = 80

	2	4	6
×		3	8
1	9	6⁴	8³
7¹	3¹	8	0
9	3	4	8
	1	1	

2·46 × 38 is equivalent to 246 × 38 ÷ 100.
This equals 9348 ÷ 100, which is 93·48.
2·46 × 38 = 93·48

Challenge 3

Find the answers to these problems.

a The sewing and fabric shop sells reels of blue and red ribbon each with 90 metres of ribbon on them. The blue ribbon is cut into pieces 2·25 metres in length. The red ribbon is cut into lengths of 1·25 metres. How many more pieces of red ribbon will there be?

b Bags of 10 buttons cost €6.90. How much would it cost to buy 55 buttons? How much change would I receive from €50?

c A length of fabric measures 5·67 m by 38 m. What is the area of the fabric?

d Liz bought three bags of sequins and a reel of cotton. The total cost was €25.40. The reel of cotton cost €3.56. How much did each bag of sequins cost?

e Ben bought 26 blue zips and 39 purple zips. He spent €247.39 altogether. Purple zips cost €4.01 each. How much does one blue zip cost?

f Jim has €100. He wants to buy 6 m of elastic at a cost of €3.54 per metre and 17 m of fabric at a cost of €6.29 per metre. How much more money does he need?

Unit 10, Week 1, Lesson 4

Solving word problems (4)

- Solve problems involving addition, subtraction, multiplication and division
- Interpret remainders according to the context

Challenge 1

Multiply each pair of numbers to find the number above. The first one has been done for you.

a) 9·6 — 8, 1·2
b) ☐ — 7, 0·9
c) ☐ — 6, 0·08
d) ☐ — 9, 3·7
e) ☐ — 4·3, 6

f) ☐ — 14, 0·07
g) ☐ — 52, 0·3
h) ☐ — 19, 0·09
i) ☐ — 30, 0·8
j) ☐ — 6·5, 6

k) ☐ — 26, 0·07
l) ☐ — 38, 0·3
m) ☐ — 11, 0·11
n) ☐ — 25, 0·07
o) ☐ — 9·8, 0·1

Challenge 2

Use the information below to work out the answer to each of these questions, rounding your answers where appropriate. Remember to use estimation to check your answers.

Biscuits:
€5.26 box

Chocolates:
€4.58 box

Pizza:
€9.38 each

Apples:
€1.47 pack of 3

Cupcakes:
€2.56 each

Soft drinks pack of 6:
€4.28

34

a Holly buys one dozen cupcakes. What is the total cost?

b Cupcakes are sold in packs of a dozen. The bakery department has 2308 cupcakes to sell. How many packs can they make?

c If you buy 14 boxes of biscuits and 25 boxes of chocolates, how much do you spend?

d How much less does a box of chocolates cost than a box of biscuits?

e Gemma has invited 73 people to a party.
   i How many packs of soft drinks will she need to buy so that each guest can have one can?
   ii How much will she pay for these packs in total?

f If you buy 2 dozen apples altogether, what is the total cost?

g If you buy one of each item, how much money will you need?

h How much change from €100 would you receive if you bought 37 cupcakes?

i If you buy one pizza you get another one half price. If you buy 6 pizzas and pay with a €50 note, how much change will you receive?

j Apples come in packs of 3. Jerzy is making 13 apple pies and needs 4 apples for each pie.
   i How many packs does he need to buy?
   ii How much will he pay in total?

k A pack of one dozen cupcakes costs €25. How much money would you save by buying them in a pack rather than as 12 single items?

l There are 439 apples altogether.
   i How many packs of 3 can be made?
   ii If the supermarket sells half of the packs in one day, how much money would they take?

Challenge 3

Make up your own word problems to match these calculations using the items in the pictures in Challenge 2.

a 20 − (12 × €1.47)
b (€4.28 ÷ 4) × 6
c (10% × €5.26) × 6
d €2.56 × 12 + €4.58 × 11 + €4.28 × 6
e €100 ÷ €9.38
f €50 < ☐ × €1.47

Unit 10, Week 2, Lesson 1

Fractions, factors and multiples (2)

- Use common factors to simplify fractions
- Use common multiples to express fractions in the same denomination

Challenge 1

1 Simplify these fractions.

a $\frac{8}{10}$ b $\frac{10}{20}$ c $\frac{15}{25}$ d $\frac{9}{12}$ e $\frac{20}{28}$

f $\frac{12}{18}$ g $\frac{16}{24}$ h $\frac{24}{30}$ i $\frac{22}{26}$ j $\frac{21}{35}$

Example

$\frac{8}{14} \rightarrow \div 2 = \frac{4}{7}$

Both the numerator and the denominator have a factor of 2 so if I divide them both by 2 I get the simplified fraction $\frac{4}{7}$.

2 Write five fractions for your partner to simplify. Make sure you know the answers!

Challenge 2

1 Simplify these fractions in two different ways.

a $\frac{30}{40}$ b $\frac{28}{36}$ c $\frac{20}{40}$ d $\frac{18}{36}$ e $\frac{32}{44}$

f $\frac{18}{24}$ g $\frac{36}{44}$ h $\frac{45}{60}$ i $\frac{27}{45}$ j $\frac{48}{64}$

Example

$\frac{20}{30} \rightarrow \div 2 = \frac{10}{15} \rightarrow \div 5 = \frac{2}{3}$

$\frac{20}{30} \rightarrow \div 10 = \frac{2}{3}$

If I use the highest common factor, which is 10, I get the simplest fraction in one step.

2 Choose two of these fractions and change them to fractions with the same denominator. Do this ten times. Fractions can be used more than once.

36

3 Using the fractions in Question 2, can you find any sets of three fractions that can be changed to fractions with the same denominator?

4 Write three fractions that would simplify to the fractions below. Use your knowledge of multiples.

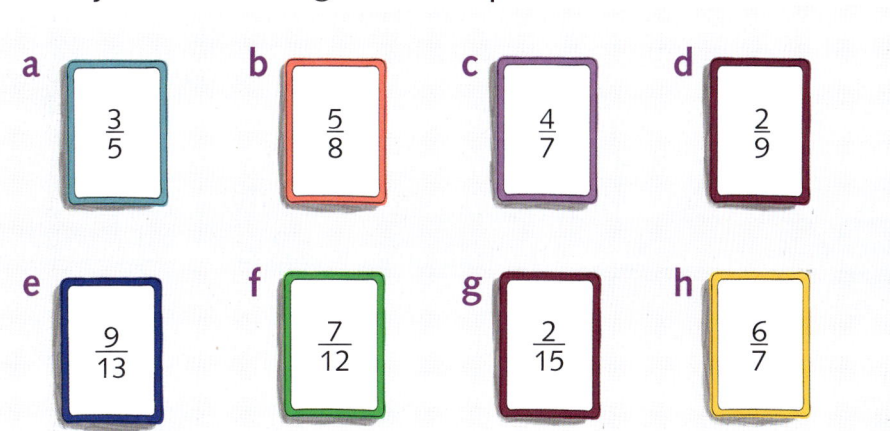

a $\frac{3}{5}$

b $\frac{5}{8}$

c $\frac{4}{7}$

d $\frac{2}{9}$

e $\frac{9}{13}$

f $\frac{7}{12}$

g $\frac{2}{15}$

h $\frac{6}{7}$

Challenge 3

1 Why does the mathematical rule for simplifying fractions state that you should use the highest common factor of the numerator and denominator?

2 Work with a partner.
- Roll the dice four times and record your digits. If you roll a 0, count it as a 10.
- Use the digits to make two proper fractions.
- Look at the denominators. Convert the fractions to two fractions with the same denominator.
- Repeat three times.
- Now roll the dice six times and make three fractions. Convert these to three fractions with the same denominator.
- Repeat three times.

You will need:
• 0–9 dice

Unit 10, Week 2, Lesson 2

Adding and subtracting fractions (2)

Add and subtract fractions with different denominators and mixed numbers, using the concept of equivalent fractions

Challenge 1

1 Work out these fraction addition and subtraction calculations.

Remember with subtraction, you may need to change the first fraction even after you have made it into an equivalent fraction with a common denominator.

a $13\frac{1}{2} + 9\frac{3}{5}$

b $17\frac{2}{3} + 16\frac{3}{4}$

c $23\frac{1}{2} - 12\frac{1}{3}$

d $21\frac{4}{6} + 17\frac{2}{9}$

e $25\frac{3}{4} - 15\frac{7}{8}$

f $27\frac{2}{5} - \frac{1}{2}$

g $20\frac{7}{8} + 21\frac{3}{4}$

h $28\frac{4}{5} - 10\frac{1}{3}$

i $22\frac{2}{6} + 19\frac{1}{4}$

j $30\frac{1}{3} - 14\frac{5}{9}$

2 Work out these word problems.

a In my race I was in third place for $\frac{1}{4}$ of it, second place for $\frac{1}{3}$ of it, and then I was in the lead for the rest. For what fraction of the race was I in the lead?

b To prepare for the race, I ate a meal the night before which was $\frac{3}{5}$ carbohydrate and $\frac{1}{3}$ protein. The rest was vegetables. What fraction of my meal was vegetables?

c I started the race with a full water bottle. I drank $\frac{5}{8}$ and shared $\frac{1}{4}$ with my friend. What fraction of the water was left at the end of the race?

d My running shirt is red, white and green. It is $\frac{1}{2}$ white and $\frac{2}{5}$ red. What fraction of my shirt is green?

Challenge 2

1. Work out these fraction addition and subtraction calculations. Write each answer in its simplest form.

   a $36\frac{1}{2} - 25\frac{4}{5}$ b $31\frac{2}{6} - 19\frac{3}{4}$ c $28\frac{4}{9} + 20\frac{5}{6}$ d $33\frac{3}{7} + 21\frac{1}{2}$ e $28\frac{1}{10} - 11\frac{2}{3}$

   f $42\frac{2}{3} + 18\frac{5}{7}$ g $46\frac{2}{6} - 31\frac{4}{5}$ h $29\frac{7}{10} + 37\frac{1}{4}$ i $35\frac{1}{4} - 26\frac{3}{5}$ j $43\frac{4}{9} + 21\frac{7}{12}$

2. Work out these word problems.

   a In my next race I was in third place for $\frac{2}{5}$ of it, second for $\frac{2}{6}$ of it and then I was in the lead for the rest. For what fraction of the race was I in the lead?

   b I started the race with a full water bottle. I drank $\frac{4}{9}$ and shared $\frac{2}{5}$ with my friend. What fraction of the water was left at the end of the race?

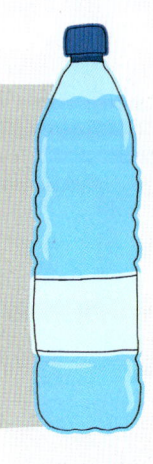

   c My running shirt is blue, yellow and orange. It is $\frac{5}{8}$ blue and $\frac{1}{6}$ orange. What fraction of my shirt is yellow?

   d When I was training for my race, I ran $7\frac{3}{4}$ km on one day and $12\frac{3}{5}$ km the next day.

   i How far did I run altogether?

   ii How much further did I run on the second day?

   e After my race, I went out for pizza with my friends. We ordered 4 pizzas. I ate $1\frac{3}{10}$ of them, Sandy ate $1\frac{3}{4}$ and Chris ate the rest. How much did Chris eat?

Challenge 3

1. After a race, €45 000 had been raised for four different charities. $\frac{2}{10}$ was given to a children's charity, $\frac{1}{3}$ to a homeless charity, $\frac{2}{5}$ to a sports charity and the rest to an animal charity.

   a What fraction did the animal charity receive?

   b How much money did each charity receive?

   c One running club raised $\frac{2}{9}$ of the money and another running club raised $\frac{1}{12}$ of the money. How much did each of these two clubs raise for charity?

2. Write your own fraction problem about how money was raised for charity. Give it to a partner to work out.

Unit 10, Week 2, Lesson 3

Fraction multiplication problems

Multiply simple pairs of proper fractions, writing the answer in its simplest form

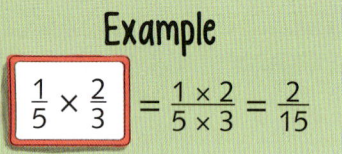

Challenge 1

1 Multiply each pair of fractions together.

Example
$\frac{1}{5} \times \frac{2}{3} = \frac{1 \times 2}{5 \times 3} = \frac{2}{15}$

a $\frac{1}{6} \times \frac{1}{2}$
b $\frac{1}{2} \times \frac{1}{4}$
c $\frac{1}{7} \times \frac{1}{3}$
d $\frac{1}{5} \times \frac{1}{2}$
e $\frac{1}{4} \times \frac{1}{3}$

f $\frac{2}{5} \times \frac{1}{3}$
g $\frac{2}{3} \times \frac{2}{4}$
h $\frac{1}{8} \times \frac{2}{3}$
i $\frac{2}{5} \times \frac{3}{4}$
j $\frac{3}{5} \times \frac{1}{5}$

2 Julie is going to make a cake but she only wants to use $\frac{1}{2}$ of the ingredients. Work out how much of each ingredient she needs.

Cake Recipe
$\frac{2}{3}$ cup of flour
$\frac{3}{4}$ cup of sugar
$\frac{1}{2}$ cup of butter
$\frac{1}{3}$ teaspoon of salt

Challenge 2

1 Multiply each pair of fractions together, writing the answer in its simplest form.

Example
$\frac{3}{5} \times \frac{4}{6} = \frac{3 \times 4}{5 \times 6} = \frac{12}{30} = \frac{2}{5}$

a $\frac{3}{4} \times \frac{2}{5}$
b $\frac{2}{6} \times \frac{3}{7}$
c $\frac{3}{8} \times \frac{1}{2}$
d $\frac{4}{9} \times \frac{3}{6}$
e $\frac{5}{10} \times \frac{2}{4}$

f $\frac{1}{12} \times \frac{4}{5}$
g $\frac{7}{8} \times \frac{2}{3}$
h $\frac{6}{10} \times \frac{2}{6}$
i $\frac{5}{7} \times \frac{3}{7}$
j $\frac{3}{4} \times \frac{6}{8}$

2 Jonny is hungry. In the fridge he finds:

- $\frac{3}{8}$ of a pizza
- $\frac{3}{4}$ of a cake
- $\frac{4}{5}$ of a litre of milk
- $\frac{2}{3}$ of a bag of carrots

Write the answer to each of these problems in their simplest form.

a If he takes $\frac{1}{4}$ of each remaining amount, what fraction of the whole item will he have taken?

b If he eats half of each remaining amount, what fraction of each whole amount will be left?

c If he eats $\frac{2}{6}$ of each remaining amount, how much will he have eaten?

Challenge 3

For the following questions record your answers in a table like the one below.

	Sunday	Monday	Tuesday	Wednesday
Fraction of cereal eaten	$\frac{2}{10}$			
Fraction of cereal left	$\frac{8}{10}$			

On Sunday night the box of cereal had $\frac{8}{10}$ left in it.

a On Monday morning, Josie got up and ate some of the cereal. She ate $\frac{1}{4}$ of what was there and left $\frac{3}{4}$.

  i What fraction of the whole box of cereal did she eat?
  ii What fraction of the whole box of cereal did she leave?

b On Tuesday she ate $\frac{1}{2}$ of what was there and left $\frac{1}{2}$.

  i What fraction of the whole box of cereal did she eat?
  ii What fraction of the whole box of cereal did she leave?

c On Wednesday she ate $\frac{4}{6}$ of what was there, and left $\frac{2}{6}$.

  i What fraction of the whole box of cereal did she eat?
  ii What fraction of the whole box of cereal did she leave?

d Compare how much cereal was in the box on Sunday night to how much was in the box on Wednesday night.

Unit 10, Week 2, Lesson 4

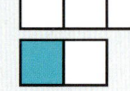

Fraction division problems

Divide proper fractions by whole numbers

Example

$$\frac{2}{6} \div 4 = \frac{2}{6 \times 4} = \frac{2}{24} = \frac{1}{12}$$

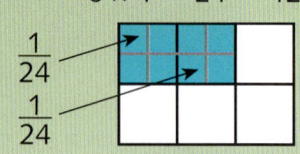

Challenge 1

1. Work out these fraction division calculations.

   a $\frac{2}{3} \div 4$ 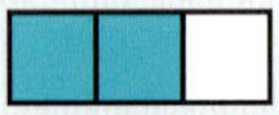
   b $\frac{1}{6} \div 3$ 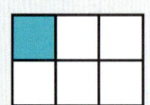
   c $\frac{2}{5} \div 3$ 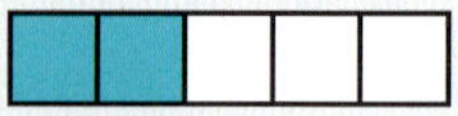
   d $\frac{3}{4} \div 2$ 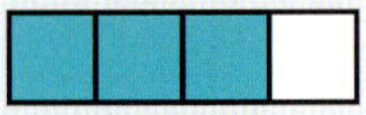
   e $\frac{1}{2} \div 5$
   f $\frac{2}{6} \div 3$ 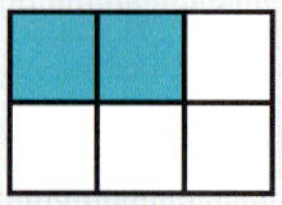
   g $\frac{3}{5} \div 4$ 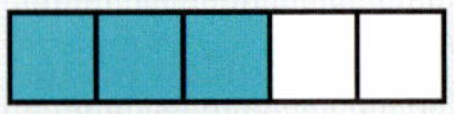
   h $\frac{3}{8} \div 2$ 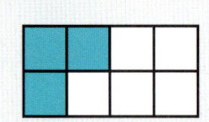
   i $\frac{4}{6} \div 3$

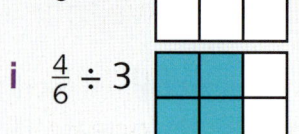

2. Four friends have these pizzas to share. How much of each pizza will each of them get?

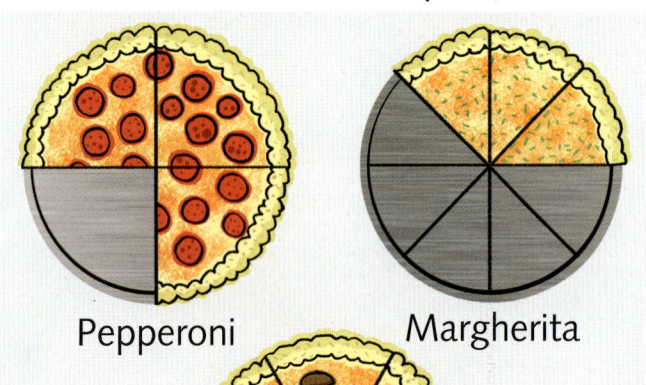

   Pepperoni   Margherita 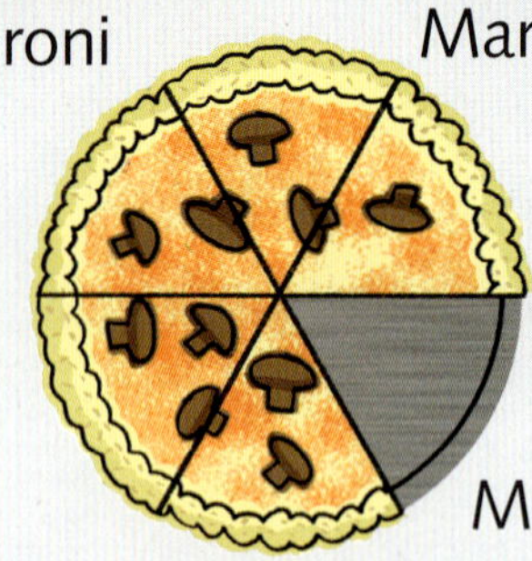   Mushroom

Challenge 2

1. Work out these fraction division calculations. Make sure your answers are simplified.

   a $\frac{3}{4} \div 5$
   b $\frac{5}{8} \div 4$
   c $\frac{6}{10} \div 3$
   d $\frac{3}{7} \div 2$
   e $\frac{4}{9} \div 3$
   f $\frac{6}{8} \div 4$
   g $\frac{4}{5} \div 3$
   h $\frac{8}{10} \div 5$
   i $\frac{3}{5} \div 9$
   j $\frac{9}{10} \div 6$
   k $\frac{11}{12} \div 3$
   l $\frac{2}{9} \div 5$

2. Choose one of the calculations from Question 1 and draw a diagram to go with it.

3 Work out these word problems.

  a Gemma has a piece of string. She cuts it so that she has $\frac{6}{8}$ of it and gives the rest to her brother. She uses her part to tie up five plants in her garden. What fraction of the original length of string does she use on each plant?

  b The Cooper family have $\frac{5}{7}$ of a cake left.
     i   What fraction of the whole cake will each of them get if they share it equally?
     ii Dad says, "As I made the cake, I think I should get extra, so count me as two people." How much would they each get if they agreed to do this?

  c Six cats have found half a fish to share.
     i   How much of a whole fish will each of them get?
     ii Luckily one of them then finds $\frac{3}{4}$ of another fish to share. What fraction of this whole fish will they get?

  d Mrs Phillips has asked five children to stay in at lunch time to discuss their maths. She has half an hour with them. What fraction of an hour will each child have if she sees each child individually for the same length of time?

Challenge 3

Work out these word problems.

  a Colin the cook has $\frac{3}{8}$ kg of sugar. He bakes 5 cakes.
     i   What fraction of a kilogram of sugar is in each cake?
     ii How many grams of sugar are in each cake?

  b Colin has made pastry. He used 0·7 kg of flour. He rolls $\frac{4}{5}$ of it out into a long strip. He cuts this into eight pieces.
     i   What fraction of the flour is in each piece?
     ii What mass of flour is in each piece?

  c Colin has $\frac{6}{10}$ left of the pie he baked yesterday. Four customers have each just ordered a slice of pie.
     i   What fraction of the whole pie would each of them get if what is left is shared equally?
     ii Before he serves his customers Colin decides he is hungry and would also like a piece of pie. What fraction of the whole pie will each of them get now?

Unit 10, Week 3, Lesson 1

Converting units of capacity

Convert between millilitres and litres using decimals up to 3 places

Challenge 1

1 Write each capacity using decimal notation.

a i $\frac{4}{10} l$ ii $\frac{4}{100} l$ iii $\frac{4}{1000} l$

b i $\frac{9}{10} l$ ii $\frac{9}{100} l$ iii $\frac{9}{1000} l$

Example

$\frac{1}{10} l = 0.1 \ l$

$\frac{1}{100} l = 0.01 \ l$

$\frac{1}{1000} l = 0.001 \ l$

2 Convert each capacity to litres using decimal notation.

a i 300 ml ii 30 ml iii 3 ml

b i 700 ml ii 70 ml iii 7 ml

c i 1600 ml ii 160 ml iii 16 ml

Example

100 ml = 0.1 l

10 ml = 0.01 l

1 ml = 0.001 l

3 Convert each capacity to millilitres.

a i 0.8 l ii 0.08 l iii 0.008 l

b i 4.5 l ii 4.05 l iii 4.005 l

Challenge 2

1 Convert the millilitres of rain water in each bucket to litres then round your answer to 1 decimal place.

Example

4545 ml = 4.545 l ≈ 4.5 l

a 5727 ml  b 8070 ml  c 3704 ml

d 16 364 ml  e 18 095 ml  f 11 507 ml

44

2 Convert each capacity to millilitres.

   a 4·9 l   b 4·49 l   c 9·04 l   d 0·94 l   e 40·909 l   f 94·004 l

3 For each statement, work out the answer to each part and write whether the statement is true or false.

   a $\frac{1}{2}$ of 3 l > $\frac{1}{4}$ of 5 l
   b $\frac{1}{2}$ of 1·5 l < $\frac{1}{4}$ of 2 l
   c $\frac{1}{3}$ of 1 l > $\frac{2}{3}$ of 900 ml
   d $\frac{1}{4}$ of 1 l < $\frac{1}{5}$ of 750 ml
   e $\frac{1}{3}$ of 1·8 l > $\frac{3}{4}$ of 1200 ml
   f $\frac{4}{5}$ of 4 l < 10 000 ml

4 Copy and complete this pattern as far as you can go.

   10 litres − 999 ml = 9·001 litres
   9·001 litres − 999 ml = ☐ litres
   ☐ litres − 999 ml = ☐ litres

5 You pour one or two of the amounts of water on the right into an empty 1 litre measuring jar. Write in litres the ten different amounts of water that your jar could now have in it.

   25 ml   0·1 l   50 ml   0·25 l

Challenge 3

Dr Davies has four measuring jars labelled A, B, C and D and four test tubes labelled 1, 2, 3 and 4. Each measuring jar is filled with a different liquid and each test tube is filled with a different chemical. She transfers the liquid from one measuring jar and the chemical from one test tube into an empty jug and mixes them together. How many different combinations of liquid and chemical can she make?

Unit 10, Week 3, Lesson 2

Maritime problems

Convert between units of capacity to solve problems using decimal notation

Challenge 1

Each goldfish needs a minimum of 9 litres of water.

1. How many goldfish can be kept in the tanks at the marine centre with these capacities:

   a 90 litres   b 135 litres   c 180 litres   d 216 litres

2. What is the capacity in litres for the tank that the marine centre will need for:

   a 12 goldfish?   b 25 goldfish?

3. The water level in a tank for 10 goldfish has fallen to 87·25 litres. How many litres of water must be added to the tank to bring it up to the minimum capacity for the goldfish?

Challenge 2

1. Andy sells motor boat fuel and refuels boats. He writes each sale in his record book. Copy and complete Andy's entry.

Boat	Meter reading at fuel pump (*l*)		Fuel sold (*l*)
	Before sale	After sale	
Sea Wind	6658	6756	98
Sea Breeze	6756	6930	
Sea Eagle	6930		158
Sea Sprite		7225	137
Sea Hawk		7391	166

2. Water is leaking from a tap at the marine centre at the rate of 5 ml per second.

   a If a 1 litre jug is placed under the tap, how many seconds will it take to fill the jug?

   b If the tap continues to leak at the same water-flow rate, how much water will be lost:

   i in one hour?   ii in one day?

3 The drinks machine at the marine centre cafe mixes 200 ml of syrup with 800 ml of water.

   a How many litres of water are needed to mix with 4500 ml of syrup?

   b How many litres of syrup are needed to mix with 64 litres of water?

4 The Sea Queen has two fuel tanks.

Tank 1 1076·175 *l*

Tank 2 895·358 *l*

   a How many litres of fuel altogether are in the Sea Queen's tanks?

   b How much more fuel is in Tank 1 than in Tank 2?

   c The Sea Queen draws alongside to refuel. It needs 4500 litres altogether for the day's trip to the island. How many litres of fuel are added to Tank 1 and Tank 2 so that each tank holds the same amount?

Challenge 3

Tanya is a marine biologist. She filled ten 500 ml bottles with samples of sea water. She capped the ten bottles and placed them in a rack made up of 25 sections so that no line (horizontal, vertical or diagonal) had more than 1 litre of liquid.

Use 1 cm squared paper to mark off a 5 × 5 square grid. Draw circles in the grid to show how Tanya could have placed her ten bottles in the rack. Write a statement explaining your reasoning.

You will need:
- 1 cm squared paper
- ruler

Unit 10, Week 3, Lesson 3

Volume of cubes and cuboids

Calculate the volume of cubes and cuboids using the rule V = lbh

Challenge 1

1. Each cube is made with 1 cm³ cubes. Calculate the volume of these cubes using the rule V = lbh.

   A   B   C

   Example

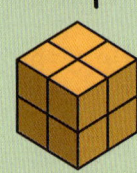

   V = lbh
   = 2 × 2 × 2
   = 8 cm³

2. The arrows show the length, breadth and height of each cuboid. Calculate the volume of these cuboids using the rule V = lbh.

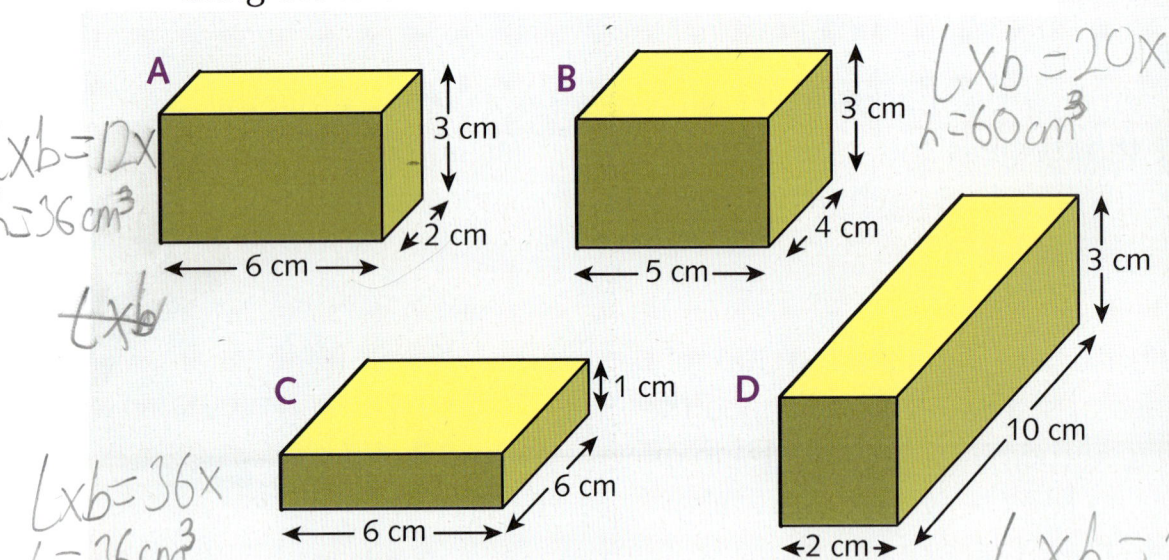

   A: 6 cm × 2 cm × 3 cm — l×b=12×, h=36cm³

   B: 5 cm × 4 cm × 3 cm — l×b=20×, h=60cm³

   C: 6 cm × 6 cm × 1 cm — l×b=36×, h=36cm³

   D: 10 cm × 2 cm × 3 cm — l×b=20×h=60cm³

   Example

   3 cm, 5 cm, 2 cm

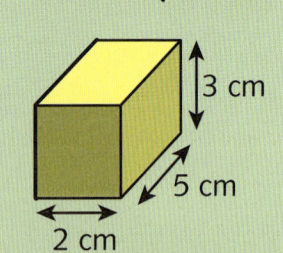

   V = lbh
   = 5 × 2 × 3
   = 30 cm³

Challenge 2

1. Calculate the volume of these cubes and cuboids using the rule V = lbh.

   A: 10 cm × 4 cm × 3 cm — l×b=40×h=120cm³

   B: 10 cm × 7 cm × 4 cm — l×b=70×h=280cm³

   C: 10 cm × 5 cm × 5 cm — l×b=50×h=250cm³

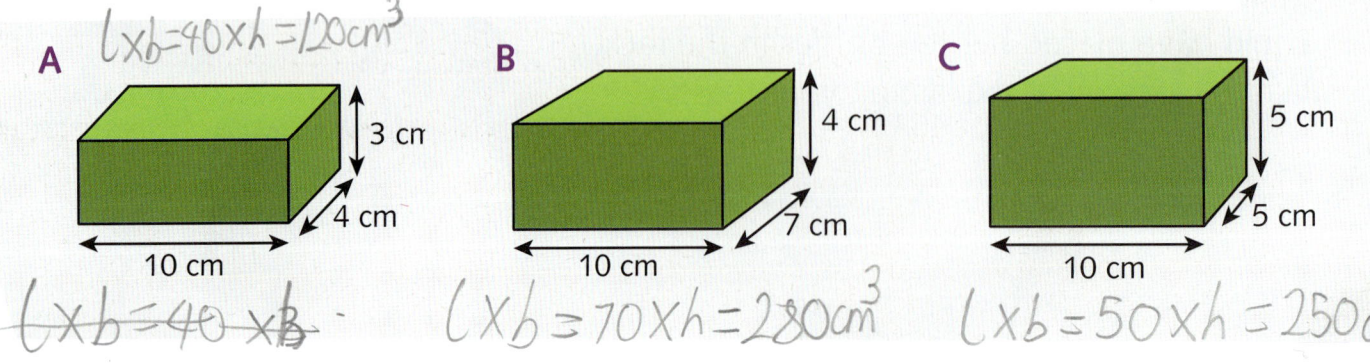

2. All 6 backpacks were loaded into the back of the minivan. Use the answers in your table for Question 1 to calculate the total mass of the 6 backpacks to the nearest kilogram.

3. Find the difference in grams between the backpacks of these children.

   a Oscar and Terry   b Mina and Steve   c Julie and Abby

4. Which three backpacks have the same combined mass as the combined mass of Steve's and Abby's backpacks?

5. Use the pictures below to answer the questions.

   a For each of the fruits, find the approximate mass of:

   i 1 fruit in grams   ii 10 fruits in kilograms   iii 100 fruits in kilograms

   b Mina put 2 apples and 1 banana into her lunch box. What was the total mass of her fruit in kilograms?

Challenge 3

Three spaniel puppies have a combined mass of 11·9 kg.

- Harry is 0·4 kg heavier than Holly.
- Holly is 200 g heavier than Heather.

What is the mass of each puppy in kilograms?

49

Unit 6, Week 3, Lesson 4

Newspaper problems

Convert between grams and kilograms to solve problems

This tables gives the mass of one copy of four daily newspapers and two Sunday newspapers.

Newspaper	Echo	Express	Globe	Times	Post on Sunday	Sunday News
Mass (g)	275	310	250	400	400	500

Challenge 1

Copy and complete the table showing the mass in kilograms for 1, 10 and 100 copies of each of the daily newspapers.

Number of copies	Echo	Express	Globe	Times
1	0·275 kg	0·31 kg	0·25 kg	0·4 kg
10	2·75 kg			
100				

Challenge 2

1 Work out the mass in grams then in kilograms for each number of copies of the daily newspapers. Copy and complete the table below.

Newspaper	Number of copies	Total mass (g)	Total mass (kg)
Echo	20		
Express	50		
Globe	40		
Times	30		

50

2 Calculate the mass in kilograms of newspapers delivered to each house in one week.

	Address	Daily (Mon–Sat)	Sunday
a	6 Ash Avenue	Express	Sunday News
b	10 Oak Grove	Times	Post on Sunday
c	35 Rowan Road	Globe	Post on Sunday
d	15 Willow Way	Echo, Times	Sunday News

3 The newspapers in Zac's bag at the start of his paper round each day have a mass of 7·385 kg. He has 5 copies of the Echo, 6 copies of the Express and 7 copies of the Globe. The rest of his newspapers are copies of the Times.

  a How many copies of the Times does he have in his bag?

  b What is the total mass in kilograms of the daily newspapers he delivers from Monday to Saturday?

4 Alfie delivers 17 copies of the Post on Sunday and 13 copies of the Sunday News to 20 houses. What is the total mass in kilograms of his newspapers at the start of his Sunday paper round?

5 How much heavier is Alfie's set of Sunday newspapers than Zac's set of daily newspapers?

6 How many of Alfie's customers take two Sunday newspapers?

Challenge 3

1 Grace, David and Lauren each have a newspaper round. The combined mass of newspapers in their bags is 21 kg. Grace's newspapers are 600 g lighter than David's newspapers. David and Lauren have exactly the same mass of newspapers. What is the mass of each child's newspapers?

2 Make up a similar newspaper-related problem for a partner to solve.

51

Unit 7, Week 1, Lesson 1

Adding and subtracting fractions (1)

Add and subtract fractions with different denominators and mixed numbers, using the concept of equivalent fractions

Example

$$\frac{3}{5} - \frac{1}{2} = \frac{6}{10} - \frac{5}{10} = \frac{1}{10}$$

10 is a multiple of 5 and 2, so I can change them both to tenths.

Challenge 1

1. Work out each of these fraction addition and subtraction calculations. Remember to start by changing both fractions to equivalent fractions with the same denominator.

a. $\frac{3}{4} + \frac{1}{2}$ b. $\frac{2}{5} + \frac{4}{10}$ c. $\frac{4}{6} + \frac{5}{12}$ d. $\frac{2}{3} + \frac{4}{6}$ e. $\frac{7}{12} + \frac{1}{6}$

f. $\frac{8}{14} + \frac{3}{7}$ g. $\frac{1}{4} + \frac{3}{5}$ h. $\frac{3}{6} + \frac{4}{9}$ i. $\frac{1}{2} + \frac{2}{3}$ j. $\frac{4}{5} + \frac{1}{2}$

k. $\frac{3}{4} - \frac{1}{2}$ l. $\frac{4}{5} - \frac{3}{10}$ m. $\frac{2}{3} - \frac{2}{6}$ n. $\frac{9}{12} - \frac{3}{6}$ o. $\frac{11}{14} - \frac{4}{7}$

p. $\frac{3}{4} - \frac{2}{5}$ q. $\frac{5}{6} - \frac{2}{9}$ r. $\frac{1}{2} - \frac{1}{3}$ s. $\frac{3}{5} - \frac{1}{2}$ t. $\frac{5}{8} - \frac{1}{3}$

2. Look at your answers to Question 1. If any of them are improper fractions, write them as mixed numbers.

Challenge 2

1 Work out each of these mixed number calculations. Write each answer as a whole number and a proper fraction.

a $12\frac{3}{4} + 11\frac{4}{5}$
b $17\frac{4}{10} + 9\frac{3}{4}$
c $18\frac{2}{8} + 16\frac{7}{12}$
d $27\frac{7}{9} + 25\frac{4}{6}$
e $21\frac{2}{6} + 18\frac{3}{4}$
f $29\frac{5}{7} + 22\frac{3}{5}$
g $24\frac{12}{15} + 26\frac{4}{10}$
h $31\frac{3}{5} + 24\frac{4}{6}$
i $22\frac{3}{6} + 38\frac{5}{7}$
j $27\frac{3}{8} + 41\frac{1}{5}$
k $26\frac{3}{4} - 14\frac{2}{5}$
l $28\frac{9}{10} - 19\frac{3}{4}$
m $29\frac{5}{8} - 21\frac{5}{6}$
n $32\frac{3}{4} - 25\frac{2}{6}$
o $39\frac{3}{7} - 29\frac{4}{5}$
p $33\frac{2}{10} - 20\frac{8}{15}$

2 Sam has worked out the calculation on the white board incorrectly. How do you think he worked it out? What do you think he does not understand? Work out the answer correctly to make sure.

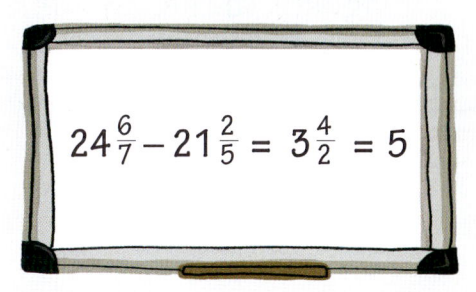

$24\frac{6}{7} - 21\frac{2}{5} = 3\frac{4}{2} = 5$

3 The tea urn in the school staffroom gets filled to the top every morning. It holds 6 litres of water. Each cup of tea or coffee uses $\frac{1}{20}$ of the water.

- At playtime, 7 people have a cup of coffee and 2 have a cup of tea.
- Then a teacher comes to fill a water jug with hot water. This uses up $\frac{1}{5}$ of the amount of water that was in the urn to start with.
- At lunchtime a teacher uses some hot water to make her soup. This uses up $\frac{1}{10}$ of a full urn.

What fraction of the water is now left in the urn?

Challenge 3

Copy and complete these addition fractions walls. Always write your answers as mixed numbers.

a $2\frac{6}{10}$ $5\frac{1}{2}$ $9\frac{2}{6}$ $4\frac{3}{4}$

b $8\frac{4}{7}$ $6\frac{1}{3}$ $7\frac{5}{6}$ $5\frac{4}{5}$

Unit 7, Week 1, Lesson 2

Dividing fractions

Divide proper fractions by whole numbers

Example

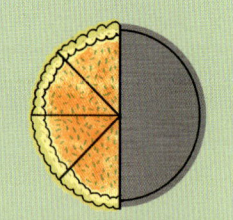

$\frac{1}{2} \div 4 = \frac{1}{8}$

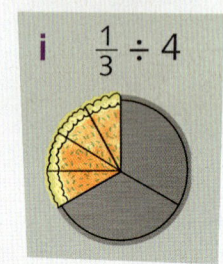

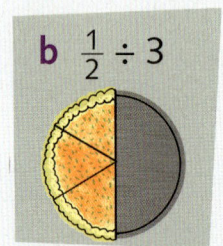

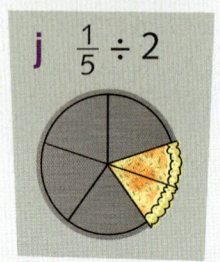

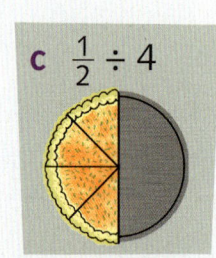

Challenge 1

In this question the fractions are represented as pizzas. Divide the fractions by the whole numbers and use the diagrams to see how much each person gets.

a $\frac{1}{2} \div 2$ 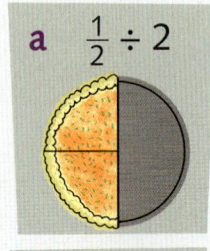
b $\frac{1}{2} \div 3$
c $\frac{1}{2} \div 4$
d $\frac{1}{4} \div 2$

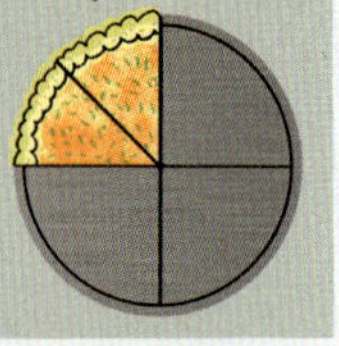

e $\frac{1}{4} \div 3$ 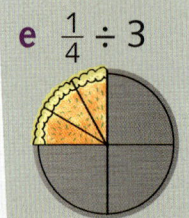
f $\frac{1}{4} \div 4$ 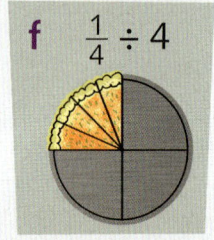
g $\frac{1}{3} \div 2$ 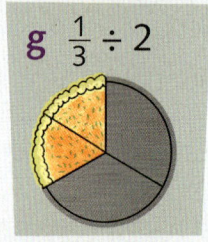
h $\frac{1}{3} \div 3$

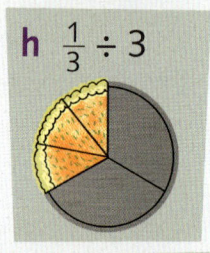

i $\frac{1}{3} \div 4$
j $\frac{1}{5} \div 2$
k $\frac{1}{5} \div 3$ 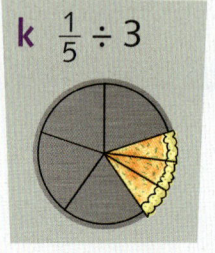
l $\frac{1}{5} \div 4$

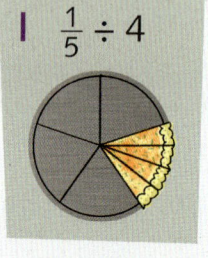

Challenge 2

1 Work out these fraction divisions. Give each answer in its simplest form.

Example

$\frac{2}{5} \div 4 = \frac{2}{20} = \frac{1}{10}$

a $\frac{2}{3} \div 3$
b $\frac{2}{5} \div 2$
c $\frac{3}{5} \div 3$
d $\frac{4}{6} \div 2$

e $\frac{2}{6} \div 3$
f $\frac{3}{4} \div 3$
g $\frac{3}{4} \div 4$
h $\frac{2}{8} \div 2$

i $\frac{5}{8} \div 3$
j $\frac{4}{10} \div 2$
k $\frac{6}{10} \div 3$
l $\frac{4}{5} \div 4$

2 Answer these word problems.

   a Lucas the chef uses $\frac{2}{3}$ kg of flour to bake 4 cakes.
      What weight of flour does he use to bake each cake?

   b Lucas uses $\frac{3}{5}$ of a bag of icing sugar to ice his 4 cakes.
      How much of the bag of icing sugar does he use to ice each cake?

   c Lucas uses $\frac{1}{6}$ of a bag of sprinkles to decorate the 4 cakes.
      How much of the bag of sprinkles does he use to decorate
      each cake?

3 Think of a time when you and your family or friends have shared something that was less than one whole. Draw a diagram and write the fraction division to go with it.

Challenge 3

1 Explain why the method for dividing fractions works. Use diagrams as part of your explanation.

2 Work out these fraction divisions.
  Give each answer in its simplest form.

   a $\frac{5}{8} \div 6$ b $\frac{4}{7} \div 5$ c $\frac{3}{4} \div 7$ d $\frac{6}{9} \div 5$

   e $\frac{8}{10} \div 6$ f $\frac{7}{11} \div 4$ g $\frac{9}{12} \div 5$ h $\frac{2}{8} \div 6$

   i $\frac{4}{10} \div 6$ j $\frac{3}{9} \div 6$ k $\frac{8}{13} \div 4$ l $\frac{10}{15} \div 6$

   m $\frac{4}{10} \div 5$ n $\frac{7}{11} \div 4$ o $\frac{3}{8} \div 3$ p $\frac{6}{14} \div 7$

3 Divide this fraction by five different whole numbers. $\frac{8}{10}$

4 Choose four calculations from Question 2 and write a word problem to go with each of them.

Unit 7, Week 1, Lesson 3

Multiplying fractions

Multiply simple pairs of proper fractions, writing the answer in its simplest form

Challenge 1

1 Work out the following multiplication calculations.

a $\dfrac{1}{2} \times \dfrac{1}{3} = \dfrac{1 \times 1}{2 \times 3} = \dfrac{\Box}{\Box}$

b $\dfrac{1}{5} \times \dfrac{1}{2} = \dfrac{1 \times 1}{5 \times 2} = \dfrac{\Box}{\Box}$

c $\dfrac{1}{3} \times \dfrac{1}{2} = \dfrac{1 \times 1}{\Box \times \Box} = \dfrac{\Box}{\Box}$

d $\dfrac{1}{4} \times \dfrac{1}{3} = \dfrac{1 \times 1}{\Box \times \Box} = \dfrac{\Box}{\Box}$

e $\dfrac{1}{6} \times \dfrac{1}{2} = \dfrac{1 \times 1}{\Box \times \Box} = \dfrac{\Box}{\Box}$

f $\dfrac{1}{3} \times \dfrac{1}{4} = \dfrac{1 \times 1}{\Box \times \Box} = \dfrac{\Box}{\Box}$

g $\dfrac{1}{5} \times \dfrac{1}{3} = \dfrac{1 \times 1}{\Box \times \Box} = \dfrac{\Box}{\Box}$

h $\dfrac{1}{4} \times \dfrac{1}{2} = \dfrac{1 \times 1}{\Box \times \Box} = \dfrac{\Box}{\Box}$

2 Work out the following multiplication calculations and give each answer in its simplest form.

a $\dfrac{2}{3} \times \dfrac{1}{4} = \dfrac{2 \times 1}{\Box \times \Box} = \dfrac{\Box}{\Box}$

b $\dfrac{2}{5} \times \dfrac{1}{2} = \dfrac{2 \times 1}{\Box \times \Box} = \dfrac{\Box}{\Box}$

c $\dfrac{1}{3} \times \dfrac{2}{6} = \dfrac{1 \times 2}{\Box \times \Box} = \dfrac{\Box}{\Box}$

d $\dfrac{2}{4} \times \dfrac{2}{5} = \dfrac{2 \times 2}{\Box \times \Box} = \dfrac{\Box}{\Box}$

e $\dfrac{3}{4} \times \dfrac{2}{3} = \dfrac{3 \times 2}{\Box \times \Box} = \dfrac{\Box}{\Box}$

f $\dfrac{4}{5} \times \dfrac{3}{4} = \dfrac{4 \times 3}{\Box \times \Box} = \dfrac{\Box}{\Box}$

Challenge 2

1 Choose 10 different pairs of fractions from below to multiply together. Work out the answer to each fraction multiplication calculation, writing your answer in its simplest form.

Example

$$\frac{2}{3} \times \frac{1}{6} = \frac{2 \times 1}{3 \times 6} = \frac{2}{18} = \frac{1}{9}$$

Stars: $\frac{2}{3}$, $\frac{4}{5}$, $\frac{3}{5}$, $\frac{1}{5}$, $\frac{1}{2}$, $\frac{2}{6}$, $\frac{2}{8}$, $\frac{1}{4}$, $\frac{4}{6}$, $\frac{3}{7}$, $\frac{5}{8}$, $\frac{3}{9}$, $\frac{3}{4}$, $\frac{2}{10}$, $\frac{1}{3}$, $\frac{1}{6}$

2 Choose one of the fraction multiplication calculations that you wrote in Question 1 and use it to write an explanation as to how to multiply pairs of fractions. Show your explanation to a partner and ask them to suggest how you might improve it.

Challenge 3

Play this game with a partner.

- Both players roll the dice four times and record the digits. 0 counts as 10.
- Use your four digits to make a fraction multiplication, like this:
- If the denominator of your answer is on the fraction wall on Resource 77: Fraction wall (2), you can colour in the appropriate number of sections on your sheet.
- Have 10 turns each.
- Work out the total fraction of the fraction wall you have coloured in.
- The winner is the player who has coloured in the most.

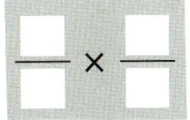

You will need:
- copies of Resource 77: Fraction wall (2)
- 0–9 dice
- coloured pencil

My fraction multiplication was:

$$\frac{6}{8} \times \frac{2}{4} = \frac{12}{32} = \frac{3}{8}$$

I can colour in three $\frac{1}{8}$ sections on the fraction wall.

57

Unit 7, Week 1, Lesson 4

Fraction problems

Solve problems involving fractions

Challenge 1

1. Work out how much pie is left. Start with one whole pie.
   - Roll the dice and read the number as a unit fraction. This will be the amount of pie that will be eaten. Roll again if you roll a 1.
   - Write the subtraction calculation to work out what fraction of the pie is left.
   - Repeat until there is less than $\frac{1}{4}$ of the pie left. Do this for three pies.

You will need:
- 1–6 dice

Example

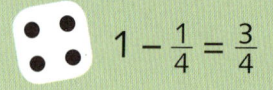

$1 - \frac{1}{4} = \frac{3}{4}$

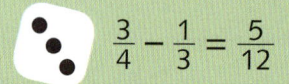

$\frac{3}{4} - \frac{1}{3} = \frac{5}{12}$

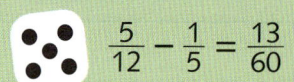

$\frac{5}{12} - \frac{1}{5} = \frac{13}{60}$

$\frac{13}{60}$ is less than $\frac{1}{4}$

2. These ingredients are for 1 apple pie. The chef wants to cook 2 pies. Work out how much of each ingredient she needs.

Apple pie ingredients
- $\frac{3}{8}$ kg butter
- $\frac{1}{4}$ kg flour
- $\frac{1}{10}$ kg sugar
- $\frac{4}{5}$ kg apples

Challenge 2

1. These ingredients are for 1 pizza. The chef wants to cook 6 pizzas. Work out how much of each ingredient he needs.

Pizza ingredients
- $\frac{3}{10}$ kg flour
- $\frac{2}{6}$ litre of water
- $\frac{3}{8}$ litre of tomato sauce
- $\frac{2}{5}$ kg mozzarella cheese
- $\frac{2}{3}$ kg mushrooms

2. These ingredients are for 2 cakes. The chef wants to cook 8 cakes. Work out how much of each ingredient he needs. Write your answers as mixed numbers.

Cake ingredients
$\frac{4}{10}$ kg sugar
$\frac{2}{7}$ kg butter
$\frac{3}{8}$ kg flour
$\frac{2}{20}$ kg cocoa powder
$\frac{1}{4}$ teaspoon baking powder
$\frac{3}{5}$ kg icing sugar

3. These pizzas are shared out between five friends. How much of a whole pizza will each person get?

a $\frac{3}{4}$ b $\frac{2}{3}$ c $\frac{4}{5}$ d $\frac{3}{5}$ e $\frac{5}{8}$

Challenge 3

1. Choose three fractions from below and add them together. Work out the answer to each fraction calculation, writing your answer in its simplest form. Make six different fraction calculations in this way.

$\frac{1}{2}$ $\frac{1}{8}$ $\frac{1}{4}$ $\frac{3}{4}$ $\frac{7}{8}$

$\frac{2}{5}$ $\frac{3}{8}$ $\frac{5}{6}$ $\frac{3}{5}$ $\frac{1}{6}$

2. Choose 3 fractions from above. Add two of the fractions together and subtract the third. Work out the answer to each fraction calculation, writing your answer in its simplest form. Make six different fraction calculations in this way.

59

Unit 7, Week 2, Lesson 1

Proportion problems

Recognise and solve proportion problems

Challenge 1

A factory produces mixed boxes of flavoured crisps. The different flavours are always produced in the same proportions. For every 2 salt and vinegar packets, there are 4 packets of plain crisps, 3 packets of cheese and onion crisps and 1 packet of prawn cocktail crisps.

a How many packets of salt and vinegar flavour are there if the total number of packets is:

　i 50?　　　ii 120?　　　iii 700?　　　iv 5000?

b What is the total number of packets of crisps if there are:

　i 12 packets of prawn cocktail?

　ii 12 packets of plain?

　iii 12 packets of cheese and onion?

　iv 12 packets of salt and vinegar?

Challenge 2

1 A pizza factory produces 4 different types of pizza. The different flavours are always produced in the same proportions. For every 4 cheese pizzas, there are 5 pepperoni pizzas, 2 mushroom pizzas and 1 chicken pizza.

a How many cheese pizzas are there if the total number of pizzas is:

　i 48?　　　ii 120?　　　iii 600?　　　iv 3600?

b What is the total number of pizzas if there are:

　i 150 cheese pizzas?　　　ii 150 pepperoni pizzas?

　iii 150 mushroom pizzas?　　　iv 150 chicken pizzas?

2   A warehouse has boxes of beanie hats.

   a   The proportion of blue beanie hats in a box is 3 out of 20. Suggest four sets of numbers of blue and other colour hats that could be in the box.

   b   For each of the total numbers of hats you calculated in **a**, choose a different colour and a different proportion out of 20 and calculate the numbers based on your new colour.

3   The proportion of red cars in the car park is always the same at 2 out of 15.

   a   How many red cars are there when there are:

      i 30 cars?   **ii** 90 cars?   **iii** 195 cars?

   b   How many cars are parked when the number of red cars is:

      i 10?   **ii** 22?   **iii** 32?

   c   When the car park is full, there are 40 red cars. What is the capacity of the car park?

Challenge 3

1   A sweet factory produces 5 different chocolate bars. The different flavours are always produced in the same proportions. For every 3 coconut flavoured bars, there are 5 honeycomb, 1 coffee, 7 orange and 4 strawberry.

   a   How many coconut flavoured bars are there if the total number of chocolate bars is:

      i 40?   **ii** 200?   **iii** 960?   **iv** 4800?

   b   What is the total number of chocolate bars if there are:

      i 100 strawberry flavoured bars?   **ii** 280 orange flavoured bars?

      iii 79 coffee flavoured bars?   **iv** 255 honeycomb flavoured bars?

2   In a town with a population of 7680 adults, 1 driver in every 9 has an advanced driver qualification. 3 out of every 4 adults in the city are drivers.
   How many advanced drivers are there in the town?

61

Unit 7, Week 2, Lesson 2

Ratio and scale factors

- Use ratios to solve problems
- Solve scale factor problems

Challenge 1

1. Write each ratio in its simplest form.

   a 6 : 12   b 6 : 18   c 24 : 30   d 28 : 21

   e 45 : 81   f 42 : 60   g 50 : 60   h 55 : 121

2. Look at the bead necklaces below.

   a In each case, write the ratio of triangular to circular beads.

   b What is the proportion of triangular beads in each necklace?

3. These two triangles are similar.

   a Find the scale factor.

   b Calculate the missing lengths of the larger triangle.

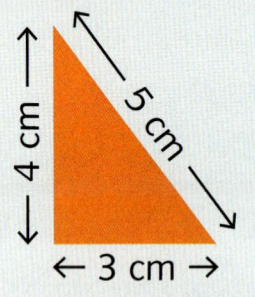

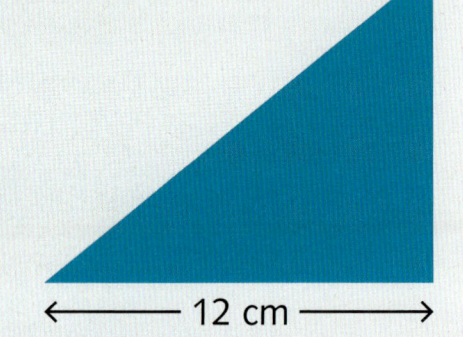

Challenge 2

1. Look at the bead necklaces below.

   a In each case, write the ratio of triangular : circular : square beads.

   b What is the proportion of triangular beads in each necklace?

62

2 Here are three similar scalene triangles. Find the scale factor for each triangle and calculate the missing lengths.

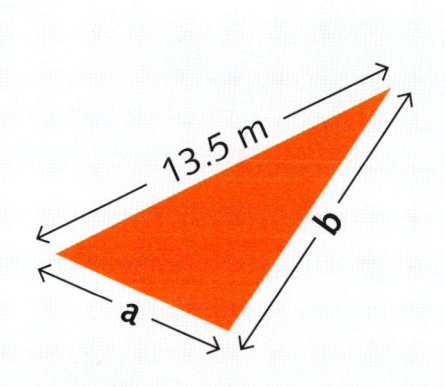

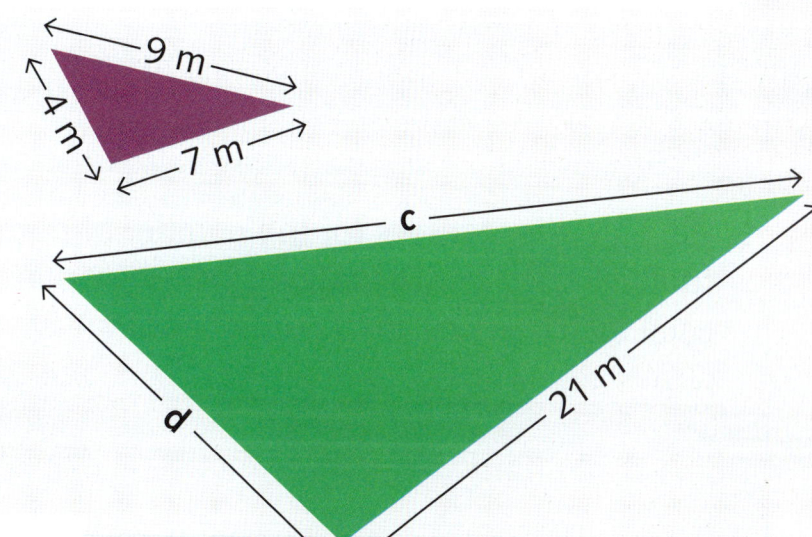

3 The numbers of children in a junior school have been recorded here.

   a Use the information in the table to calculate:

   i the number of boys and girls in each year group

   ii the number of boys in the school

   iii the number of girls in the school.

   b One new boy joins the school. What is the ratio of boys to girls in the whole school now?

Year group	Total number of children	Ratio of boys to girls
Y3	80	5 : 3
Y4	84	3 : 4
Y5	90	8 : 7
Y6	85	9 : 8

Challenge 3

You have red and blue beads.

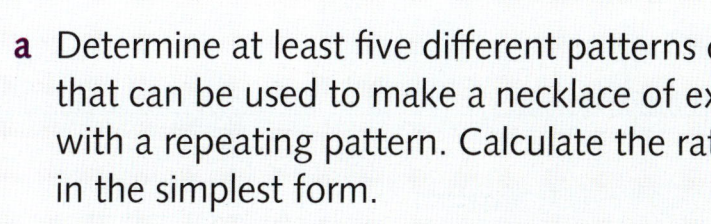

   a Determine at least five different patterns of beads that can be used to make a necklace of exactly 30 beads with a repeating pattern. Calculate the ratios of beads in the simplest form.

   b Can you list all the possible repeating patterns?

63

Unit 7, Week 2, Lesson 3

Ratio problems

Solve missing value ratio problems using multiplication and division

Challenge 1

1. Here are the statistics for the number of home supporters at five different football matches. The ratio of home supporters to away supporters is given for each match. Calculate the number of away supporters for each match.

Home supporters	48 000	72 000	55 000	63 000	39 000
Ratio of home : away supporters	8 : 1	6 : 1	10 : 1	9 : 2	13 : 2

2. Look at each pair of statements and decide if the second statement is true or false and explain why, or give the correct answer for any that are false.

   a. Grey paint is 1 part black paint to 4 parts white paint. In a 10 l tin of grey paint, there are 8 l of white paint.

   b. The ratio of boys to girls in a class is 3 : 2. In a class of 30 children, there are 12 girls.

   c. Sam spent €100 on clothes and CDs in the ratio 3 : 2. He spent €40 on clothes.

Challenge 2

1. Here are two strawberry smoothie recipes.

   a. Calculate the amount of each ingredient required for each recipe to serve 12.

   b. Which smoothie has a higher ratio of strawberry to apple?

   c. How many people can you serve one smoothie to if you have 24 oranges and 24 nectarines but unlimited quantities of the other fruits?

Strawberry and nectarine smoothie

Serves 4
- 12 strawberries
- 3 nectarines
- 4 apples

Strawberry and banana smoothie

Serves 3
- 16 strawberries
- 1 banana
- 1 orange
- 4 apples

2 Here is a recipe for Chocolate Fudge Brownies.

   a Write the following ratios in their simplest form:

      i   chocolate : butter

      ii chocolate : brown sugar

      iii chocolate : chocolate chips

      iv brown sugar : chocolate chips

   b How many servings are there if you use:

      i   15 ml vanilla extract?   ii a dozen eggs?

      iii 1 kg brown sugar?   iv 60 g butter?

> Chocolate Fudge Brownie
>
> Serves 12
>
> - 180 g chocolate
> - 120 g butter
> - 200 g brown sugar
> - 6 ml vanilla extract
> - 2 eggs
> - 180 g plain flour
> - 100 g chocolate chips

3 Look at each pair of statements and decide if the second statement is true or false. Explain why, or give the correct answer for any that are false.

   a Grey paint is 1 part black paint to 4 parts white paint. In a 2 *l* tin of paint, there is 1·6 *l* of white paint.

   b The ratio of boys to girls in a class is 4 : 5. In a class of 27 children, there are 15 girls.

   c 200 kg of sand is divided into piles in the ratio 2 : 3. The smaller pile is 80 kg.

   d The approximate ratio of time asleep : time awake for a newborn baby is 2 : 1. A baby is awake for 56 hours in a week.

Challenge 3

Look at each pair of statements and decide if the second statement is true or false.

   a Purple paint is 4 parts blue paint to 3 parts red paint. In a 3·5 *l* tin of paint, there is 1·5 *l* of red paint.

   b The ratio of boys to girls in a class is 7 : 8. In a class of 30 children, there are 16 girls.

   c Three Year 6 classes collected money for charity. The money they raised was in the ratio 7 : 6 : 5. Two of the classes raised €126 and €110.

   d 260 kg of sand is divided into piles in the ratio 6 : 7. The smaller pile is 120 kg.

Unit 7, Week 2, Lesson 4

Ratio and proportion problems

Solve problems involving unequal sharing and grouping using knowledge of fractions and multiples

Cauliflower Cheese for 4

- 1 cauliflower (about 700 g)
- 40 g butter
- 40 g plain flour
- 450 ml milk
- 100 g grated cheddar cheese
- 20 g breadcrumbs (optional)

Challenge 1

1. This cauliflower cheese recipe serves 4.

    a Write the cauliflower cheese recipe for 6 people.

    b Explain your method.

    c Discuss your method with a partner and see if you did it in the same way

2. Orange squash concentrate is mixed with water in the ratio 1 : 6 to make drinks. How much squash can be made from:

    a 200 ml of concentrate?   b 4 l of concentrate?

Challenge 2

1. A pancake recipe says that for every egg you need 3 spoonfuls of plain flour and 2 cups of milk. This is enough mixture to make 4 small pancakes.

    a Write the ingredients required for 4 eggs. How many pancakes will this make?

    b You want to make 100 pancakes for a party. Calculate the amount of ingredients required.

2. A paint company mixes paint in the following ratios:

    Puzzling purple – 4 red : 5 blue : 1 white

    Outrageous orange – 3 red : 6 yellow : 1 white

    Pretty pink – 6 red : 9 white

    Groovy grey – 3 black : 5 white

    Bold brown – 4 red : 3 blue : 1 yellow

a How many litres of each paint do you need to make 20 litres of each colour?

b Stocks of red paint are very low, with only 12 *l* left.

   i What colour should the company make to give the largest quantity?

   ii Calculate how many litres can be made.

3 A restaurant buys a box of mixed red, green and yellow peppers.

- There is a minimum of 100 peppers in every box.
- There is a maximum of 115 peppers in every box.
- The proportion of red peppers in the box is 2 out of 5.
- The ratio of yellow to green peppers is 1 : 2.

What are the possible numbers of each colour of pepper?

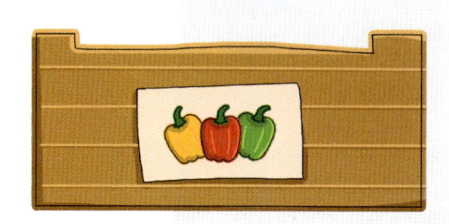

Challenge 3

Three animal charities raised money for pandas, tigers and elephants at an outdoor event in a field. The field was shared in the ratio 2 : 3 : 5 according to the amount of money each charity paid to take part. At the event, the charities then raised a total of €3000.

a How much would each charity have raised if the money they collected was in the same ratio as the area of the field they were using?

b The actual amount collected by each charity was €1000 for pandas, €800 for tigers and €1200 for elephants. Express this ratio in its simplest form.

c The tiger charity paid €150 for its space in the field. Calculate which charity made the most profit overall.

Unit 7, Week 3, Lesson 1

Water sports centre pie charts

Interpret and draw pie charts and use them to solve problems

These pie charts show the children's favourite activities at the water sports centre over four weeks. Each sector in these pie charts represents 10%.

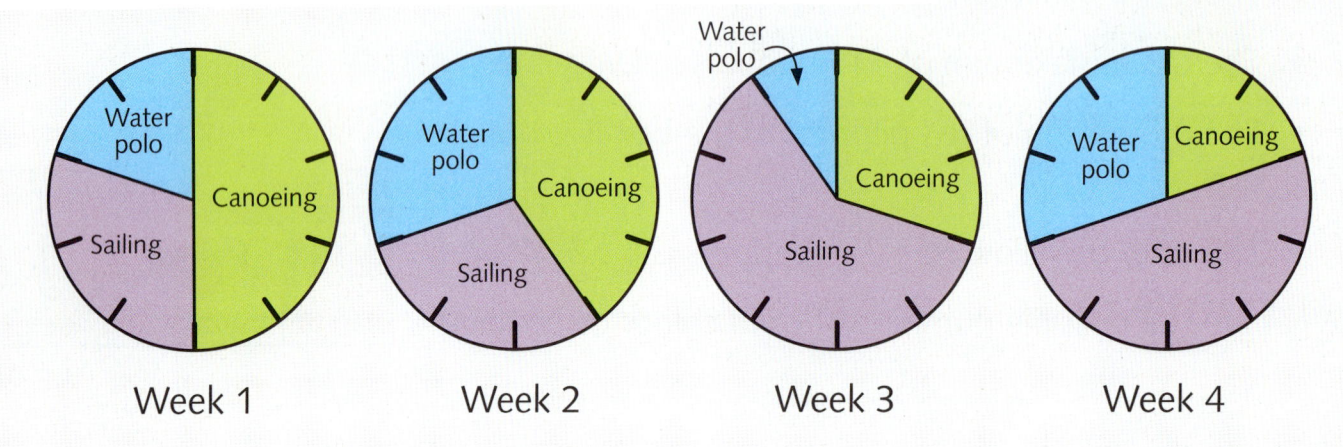

Week 1 | Week 2 | Week 3 | Week 4

Challenge 1

Copy the table below. Then use the data in the pie charts above to find the percentage of children who chose each activity as their favourite.

Activity	Week 1	Week 2	Week 3	Week 4
Canoeing	50%			
Sailing				
Water polo				

Challenges 2, 3

1 Use the information in the pie charts at the top of the page to complete the database in Resource 48: Database.

You will need:
- Resource 48: Database
- ruler
- four coloured pencils

2 Use your database to find out in which week:

   a equal numbers of children chose sailing and water polo

   b twice as many children chose sailing than canoeing

   c more children chose water polo than canoeing

   d 8 more children chose canoeing than sailing

   e 6 fewer children chose canoeing than water polo.

3 Which two weeks had the same number of children who preferred:

   a canoeing? b sailing?

4 Complete the pie charts on Resource 48: Database to show the information below for Weeks 5 and 6. Colour each pie chart and complete its key.

Week	Total number of children	Number of children choosing each activity			
		Canoeing	Sailing	Water polo	Rafting
5	60	24	18	12	6
6	60	15	24	9	12

Challenge 3

Look at your completed pie charts on Resource 48.

1 Write three statements that describe how the pie charts for Weeks 5 and 6 are similar or different from each other.

2 Write three questions about the pie charts for Weeks 5 and 6 for a partner to answer.

Unit 7, Week 3, Lesson 2

Using line graphs

Construct and use line graphs to solve problems

You will need:
- 1 cm squared paper
- ruler

Challenge 1

1 Copy the table below. Then use the relationship 8 km ≈ 5 miles to complete it.

Kilometres	0	8	16	24	32	80
Miles	0	5				

2 Use the data from the completed table in Question 1 to draw a line graph for converting between miles and kilometres. Make sure you join the points with a straight line and that your graph is big enough to extend your line to the point (80, 50).

3 Use your graph to convert these distances to kilometres.

   a 25 miles   b 30 miles   c 45 miles

4 Use your graph to convert these distances to miles.

   a 20 km   b 28 km   c 44 km

Challenge 2

You will need:
- 1 cm squared paper
- ruler

1 Copy the table below. Then use the relationship 6 minutes to travel a distance of 5 kilometres to complete it.

Time (min)	0	6	12	18	24	72
Distance (km)	0	5				

2 Use the data from the completed table in Question 1 to draw a time distance graph. Make sure you join the points with a straight line and that your graph is big enough to extend your line to the point (72, 60).

3 Find the distance travelled in: a 36 minutes   b 60 minutes

4 Find the time taken to travel: a 35 km   b 45 km

5 The graph on the right shows that a taxi driver charges €2 for a pick-up fee and €1.50 per kilometre.

Journey cost

a What is the cost for a journey of:

   i   2 kilometres?
   ii 6 kilometre?
   iii 10 kilometres?
   iv 5 kilometres?

b What distance was travelled if the fare was:

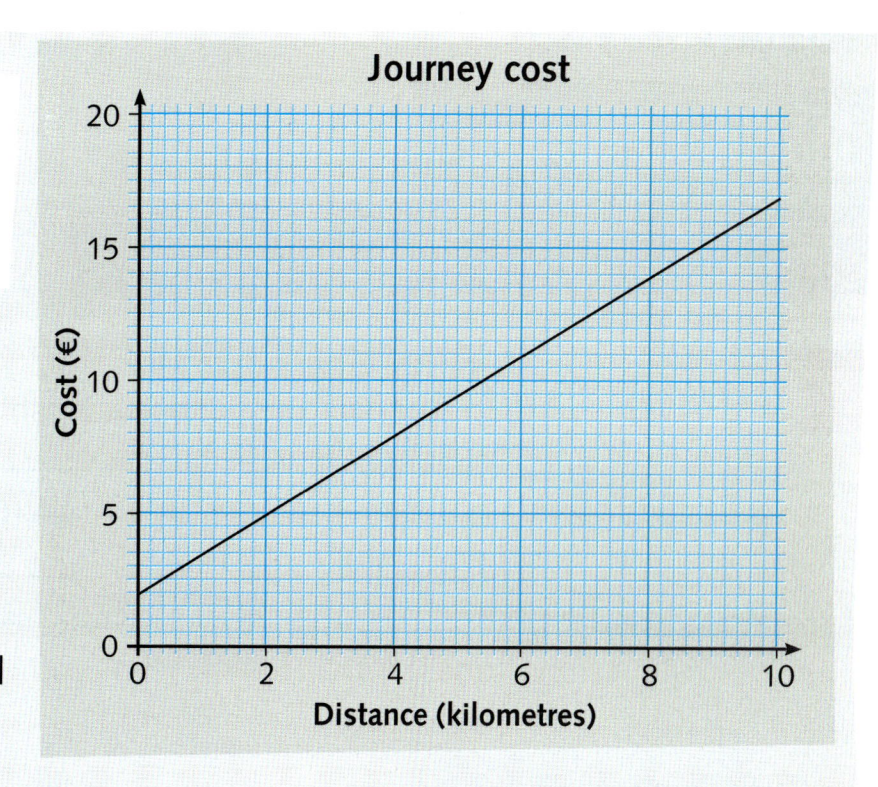

   i €12.50?   ii €15.50?

Challenge 3

A function machine converts °F to °C using the rule:

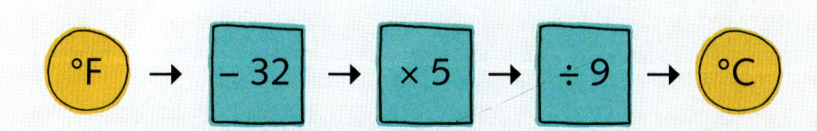

°F → − 32 → × 5 → ÷ 9 → °C

You will need:
- Resource 49: °F to °C graph paper
- 1 cm squared paper
- ruler

1 Copy the table below. Use the function machine to complete the values for °C rounded to the nearest degree.

°F	32	41	61	82	95	110
°C						

City	°F	°C
Boston	77	
Canberra	52	
Madrid	81	
Tokyo	72	
Dubai	102	
Luxor	106	
Paris	66	
Bangkok	91	

2 Plot the points on Resource 49: °F to °C graph paper and draw the conversion graph.

3 Copy the table on the right and use your graph to convert the temperatures to °C, to the nearest degree.

Unit 7, Week 3, Lesson 3

Making a survey

Collect and organise data to solve problems

Challenge 1

Work with a partner for this investigation.

How many hours did you spend watching TV after school yesterday?

- Copy the frequency table.
- Collect data from 20 people in your school and complete your frequency table.
- Write a short conclusion based on what you have found out.

Time spent watching TV	Tally	Frequency
None		
Up to 1 hour		
More than 1 hour but less than 2 hours		
2 hours or more		

Challenge 2

Work with a partner. Choose one of the following investigations to answer: Question 1 or Question 2.

You will need:
- 1 cm squared paper
- ruler

1 *How many hours did you spend playing computer games after school yesterday?*

- Copy the frequency table.
- Collect data from 20 people in your school and complete your frequency table.
- Illustrate your report with suitable diagrams or graphs and explain why you have used them.
- Write a short conclusion based on what you have found out.

Time spent playing computer games	Tally	Frequency
None		
Up to 1 hour		
More than 1 hour but less than 2 hours		
2 hours or more		

2 *Which of these activities do you do outside school?*

- Copy the frequency table.
- Collect data from 20 people in your school and complete your frequency table.
- Illustrate your report with suitable diagrams or graphs and explain why you have used them.
- Write a short conclusion based on what you have found out.

Activity	Tally	Frequency
Football		
Swimming		
Dance		
Something else		
No outside school activity		

Challenge 3

Work with a partner. Survey 20 or more people in your school and ask them two questions:

A *How much pocket money do you get per week?*

B *What do you spend most of your pocket money on?*

- Design your own frequency table for **A**. Give a choice of four responses, for example: 'None', 'Less than €2', '€2 to €5', or 'More than €5'.
- Devise a questionnaire for **B**. Give a choice of four responses, for example: 'Sweets', 'Sport', 'Music' or 'Other'.
- Illustrate your report with suitable diagrams or graphs and explain why you have used them.
- Write a short conclusion based on what you have found out.

You will need:
- 1 cm squared paper
- ruler

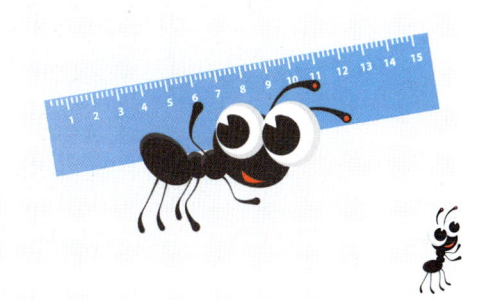

Unit 7, Week 3, Lesson 4

Finding the mean

Calculate and interpret the mean as an average of a set of data

Challenge 1

Find the mean value of each set of cards.

Example

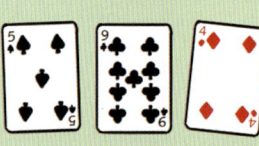

$5 + 9 + 4 = 18$

$18 \div 3 = 6$

Mean = 6

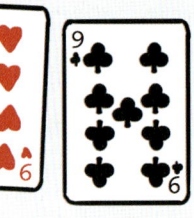

a 8, 6, 7

b 7, 2, 9

c 10, 4, 9, 9

d 5, 6, 6, 3

Challenge 2

1 Find the mean of each set of numbers.

a 4   8   12   16

b 3   9   15   21

c 5   15   25   35

d 9   11   17   23

2 Four trays of sandwiches have been prepared for lunch.

a How many sandwiches are on each tray?

b Calculate the mean number of sandwiches per tray.

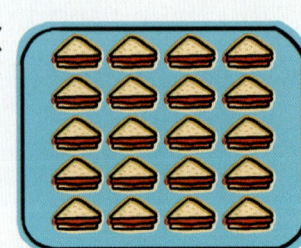

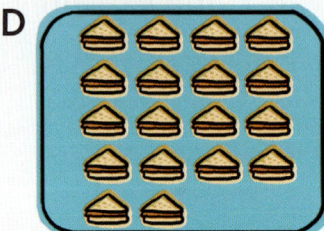

A   B   C   D

3 The table below shows the number of goals scored in six games by players in the school's netball team.

   a Find the mean number of goals scored by each player.

   b Find the mean number of goals scored per game.

Player	Number of goals					
	Game 1	Game 2	Game 3	Game 4	Game 5	Game 6
Donna	2	1	2	3	3	1
Leah	4	3	5	1	3	2
Maria	3	5	4	2	0	4
Tanya	3	6	1	3	3	5

4 The table shows the distance run by each athlete in five training sessions. Calculate the mean distance run by each athlete in one training session.

Athlete	Distance (km)
Marek	45
Jonny	32·5
Jordan	37
Simon	41·5

Challenge 3

The height of a pony is measured in hands. The table shows the height in hands of Jack, Jenny, Julie and Jingle. The mean height of the five ponies is 13 hands. What height is Joyce in hands?

Pony	Hands
Jack	15
Jenny	11
Julie	12
Jingle	13
Joyce	

Unit 8, Week 1, Lesson 1

Division HTO ÷ TO using the expanded written method

- Use the expanded written method of long division to calculate HTO ÷ TO
- Estimate and check the answer to a calculation

Challenge 1

Work out the answer to each calculation.

| 1 a 26 × 3 | 2 a 37 × 8 | 3 a 19 × 6 | 4 a 45 × 7 | 5 a 84 × 9 |
| b 26 × 30 | b 37 × 80 | b 19 × 60 | b 45 × 70 | b 84 × 90 |

| 6 a 63 × 4 | 7 a 90 × 7 | 8 a 28 × 5 | 9 a 33 × 6 | 10 a 9 × 54 |
| b 63 × 40 | b 90 × 70 | b 28 × 50 | b 33 × 60 | b 90 × 54 |

| 11 a 7 × 42 | 12 a 58 × 6 | 13 a 8 × 81 | 14 a 5 × 11 | 15 a 71 × 4 |
| b 70 × 42 | b 60 × 58 | b 81 × 80 | b 50 × 11 | b 40 × 71 |

Challenge 2

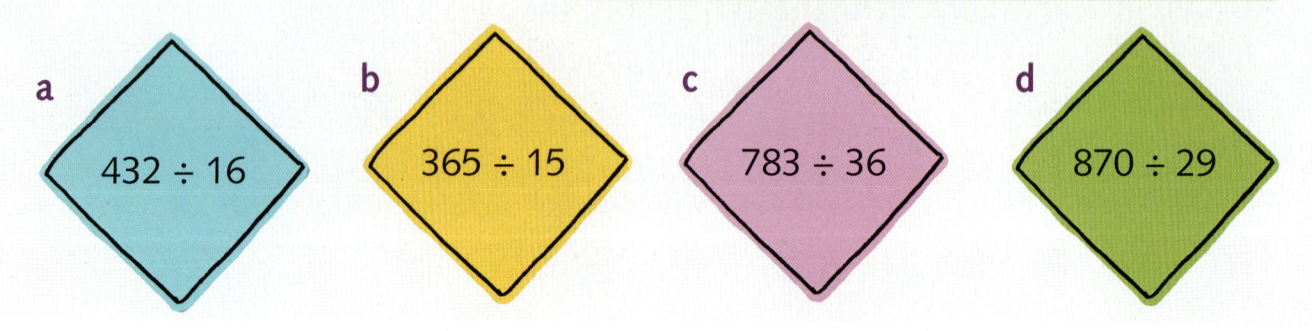

1 For each division calculation write your estimate, then use the expanded written method to work out the answer. Record any remainders as a fraction. Be sure to compare your answer with your estimate.

Example

644 ÷ 14 → 600 ÷ 10 = 60 or 600 ÷ 15 = 40

```
       H T O
         4 6
    ┌─────────
14 │ 6⁵ ¹⁴4 4
  -  5 6 0      (40 × 14)
     ─────
         8 4
  -      8 4    (6 × 14)
         ───
           0
```

a 432 ÷ 16

b 365 ÷ 15

c 783 ÷ 36

d 870 ÷ 29

76

e 686 ÷ 23
f 770 ÷ 22
g 596 ÷ 14
h 775 ÷ 25
i 836 ÷ 19
j 756 ÷ 14

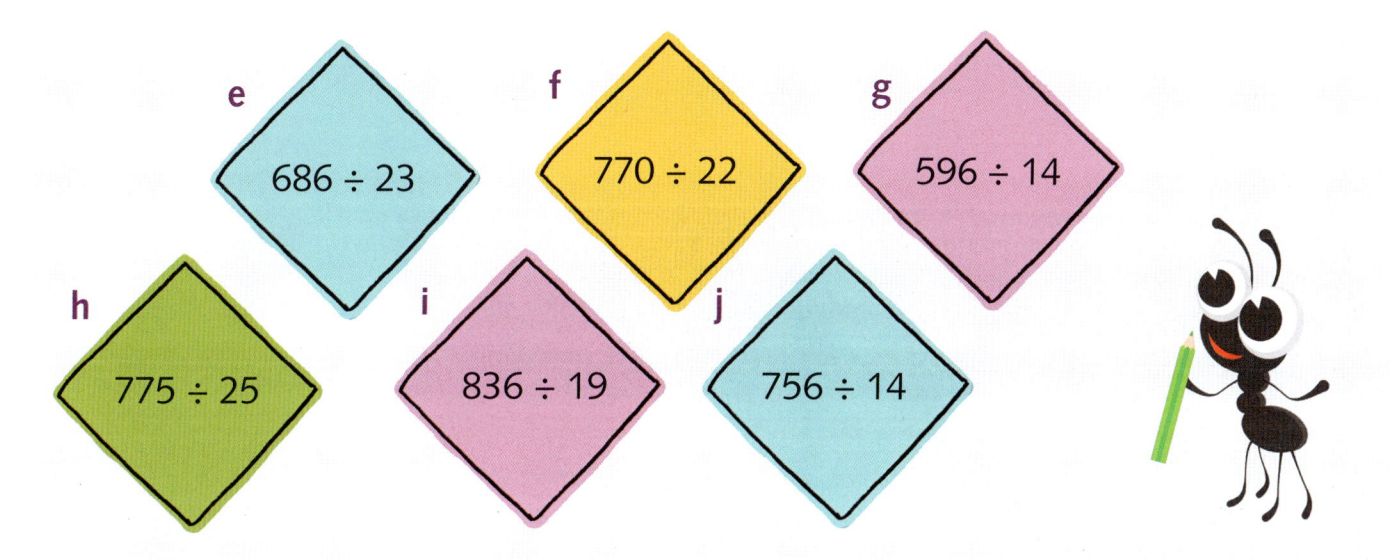

2 Play this game with a partner.

- Choose one number from each box.
- Divide the 3-digit number by the 2-digit number, and write the answer as a whole number.
- Your score is the remainder.
- Your partner checks your working, then takes a turn to choose a different pair of numbers.
- After 4 rounds, add together all your remainders. The winner is the player with the largest total.

924	561	349	294
373	835	573	602
256	787	136	728
162	448	615	819

26	54	45	97
62	89	73	38
17	43	84	99
64	51	32	76

Challenge 3

1 Find the answer to each of these problems.

a If a plane travels at 506 kilometres per hour, how far would it travel in 1 minute?

b A plane travels at 840 km per hour. If it is 196 km east of its destination, how long will it take to reach the destination?

c A car uses 882 litres of petrol in a fortnight. How many litres does it use on average per day?

d The total bill for 24 nights hotel accommodation is €936. How much does it cost per night?

2 Write down five situations when you would need to divide to find the answer.

Unit 8, Week 1, Lesson 2

Division ThHTO ÷ TO using the expanded written method

- Use the expanded written method of long division to calculate ThHTO ÷ TO
- Estimate and check the answer to a calculation

Challenge 1

Work out the answer to each calculation.

1. a 24 × 100
   b 42 × 100

2. a 67 × 100
   b 76 × 100

3. a 59 × 100
   b 95 × 100

4. a 36 × 7
   b 36 × 700

5. a 57 × 4
   b 57 × 400

6. a 49 × 9
   b 49 × 900

7. a 85 × 5
   b 85 × 500

8. a 64 × 2
   b 64 × 200

Challenge 2

1. For each division calculation write your estimate, then use the expanded written method to work out the answer. Record any remainders as a fraction. Be sure to compare your answer with your estimate.

Example

$5832 ÷ 18 \rightarrow 6000 ÷ 20 = 300$ or $5400 ÷ 18 = 300$

```
      Th H T O
          3 2 4
   18 | 5 8 3 2
      - 5 4 0 0    (300 × 18)
        ³4 ¹³3 2
      -   3 6 0    (20 × 18)
            7 2
      -     7 2    (4 × 18)
              0
```

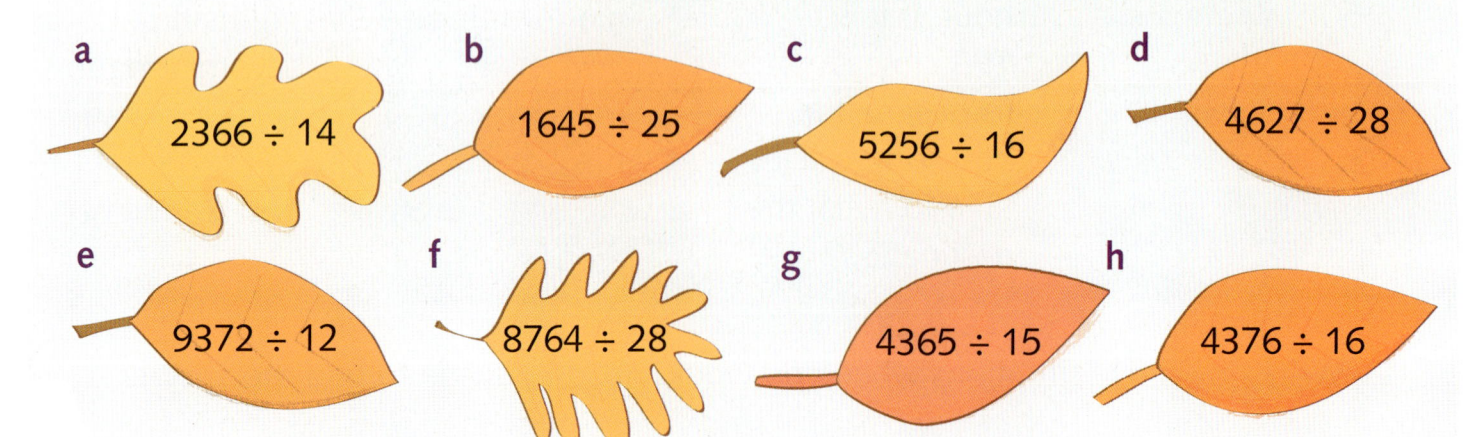

a 2366 ÷ 14

b 1645 ÷ 25

c 5256 ÷ 16

d 4627 ÷ 28

e 9372 ÷ 12

f 8764 ÷ 28

g 4365 ÷ 15

h 4376 ÷ 16

2 Play this game with a partner.

- Choose one number from each box.
- Divide the 4-digit number by the 2-digit number, and write the answer as a whole number.
- Your score is the remainder.
- Your partner checks your working, then takes a turn to choose a different pair of numbers.
- After 4 rounds, add together all your remainders. The winner is the player with the largest total.

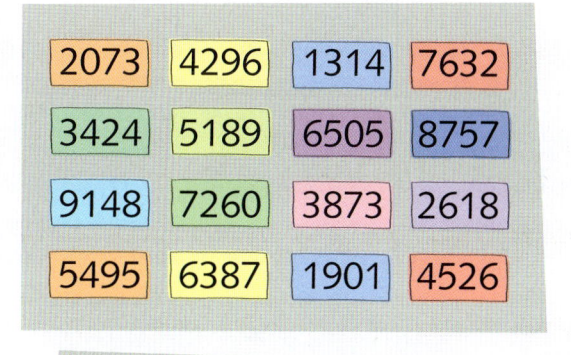

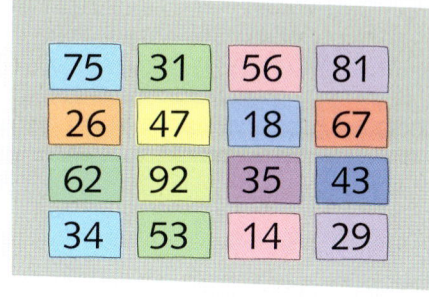

2073	4296	1314	7632
3424	5189	6505	8757
9148	7260	3873	2618
5495	6387	1901	4526

75	31	56	81
26	47	18	67
62	92	35	43
34	53	14	29

Challenge 3 The answer to five of these calculations is 49. Can you find which ones?

1225 ÷ 25

1127 ÷ 23

1104 ÷ 24

882 ÷ 18

588 ÷ 12

1296 ÷ 27

1764 ÷ 36

1034 ÷ 22

1472 ÷ 32

Unit 8, Week 1, Lesson 3

Division HTO ÷ TO using the formal written method

- Use the formal written method of long division to calculate HTO ÷ TO
- Estimate and check the answer to a calculation

Challenge 1

Work out the answers to these mentally.

1. a 150 ÷ 15
   b 360 ÷ 36
   c 620 ÷ 62
   d 240 ÷ 24
   e 310 ÷ 31

2. a 240 ÷ 12
   b 480 ÷ 24
   c 450 ÷ 15
   d 360 ÷ 18
   e 390 ÷ 13

3. a 550 ÷ 11
   b 600 ÷ 12
   c 560 ÷ 14
   d 840 ÷ 12
   e 340 ÷ 17

4. a 640 ÷ 20
   b 390 ÷ 30
   c 450 ÷ 50
   d 810 ÷ 90
   e 540 ÷ 60

Challenge 2

1. For each division calculation write your estimate, then use the formal written method to work out the answer. Record any remainders as a fraction in its simplest form. Be sure to compare your answer with your estimate.

Example

644 ÷ 14 → 600 ÷ 10 = 60 or 600 ÷ 15 = 40

```
       4 6
   14 ) 6 4 4
      - 5 6 ↓
          8 4
        - 8 4
            0
```

a 398 ÷ 24
b 645 ÷ 15
c 526 ÷ 16
d 632 ÷ 28
e 961 ÷ 17
f 676 ÷ 24
g 846 ÷ 14
h 245 ÷ 13
i 488 ÷ 24
j 475 ÷ 25
k 780 ÷ 25
l 1596 ÷ 18

80

2 Copy and complete these division calculations, writing in the missing digits.

a
```
      2 □ r □
27 | 6 0 2
   - □ 4 ↓
     ─────
       6 □
     - □ 4
       ───
         □
```

b
```
     □ 3 r □
18 | 7 8 1
   - □ 2 ↓
     ─────
       □ 1
     - □ □
       ───
         □
```

c
```
      2 □ r □
37 | 8 7 3
   - 7 □ ↓
     ─────
       1 □ 3
     - □ 1 1
       ─────
         □ □
```

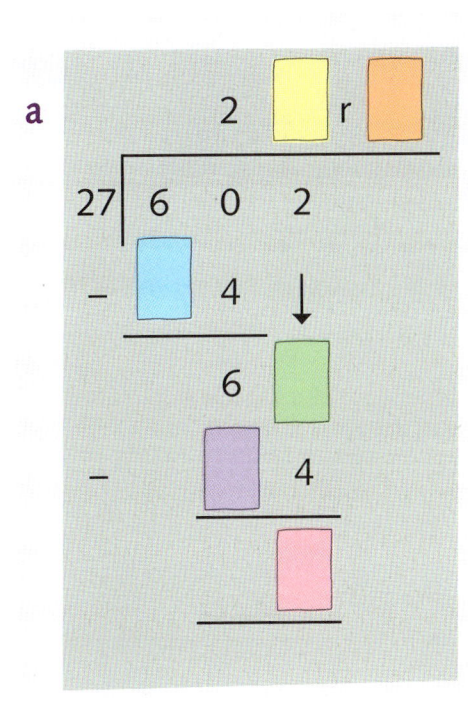

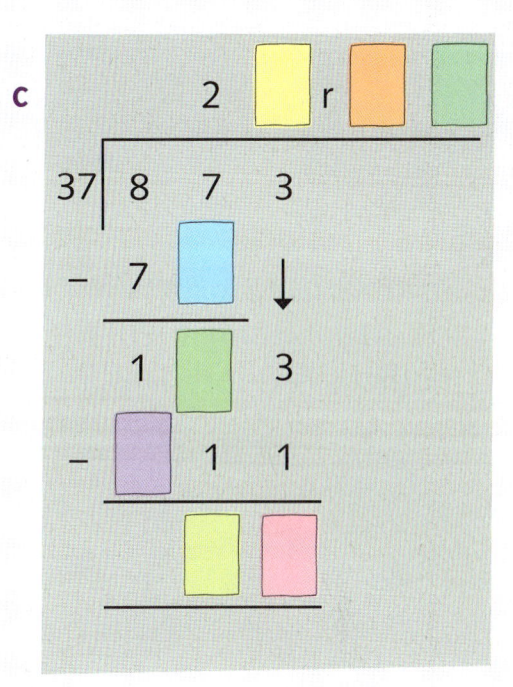

Challenge 3

Find the answer to each of these problems.

a There are 792 books. The same number of books is placed onto 18 different shelves. How many books are placed onto each shelf?

b A carton contains 672 pencils altogether. The pencils are in boxes of 12. How many boxes of pencils are there in the carton?

c 770 packed lunches are shared equally between 35 classes. How many children in each class receive a packed lunch?

d 912 playground items are shared equally among 24 classes. How many items does each class receive?

Unit 8, Week 1, Lesson 4

Division ThHTO ÷ TO using the formal written method

- Use the formal written method of long division to calculate ThHTO ÷ TO
- Estimate and check the answer to a calculation

Challenge 1

Work out the answer to each calculation using mental methods or short division.

Example

$245 ÷ 4$

$245 ÷ 4 = (240 + 5) ÷ 4$
$= 60 + 1 \text{ r } 1$
$= 61 \text{ r } 1$

```
      6 1 r 1
  4 | 2 4 5
```

a

	÷ 4
i	329
ii	154
iii	284
iv	447
v	208

b

	÷ 8
i	357
ii	435
iii	256
iv	188
v	571

c

	÷ 6
i	378
ii	488
iii	256
iv	639
v	565

d

	÷ 9
i	279
ii	549
iii	631
iv	452
v	723

Challenge 2

For each division calculation write your estimate, then use the formal written method to work out the answer. Record any remainders as a fraction in its simplest form. Be sure to compare your answer with your estimate.

Example

$5832 ÷ 18 \rightarrow 6000 ÷ 20 = 300$
or $5400 ÷ 18 = 300$

```
          3 2 4
    18 | 5 8 3 2
       - 5 4 ↓
           4 3
         - 3 6 ↓
             7 2
           - 7 2
               0
```

a 8436 ÷ 12
b 9875 ÷ 25
c 9352 ÷ 21
d 6464 ÷ 18
e 7370 ÷ 15
f 5391 ÷ 18
g 8866 ÷ 26
h 3080 ÷ 35

Challenge 3

1. Deepa is training for the marathon. Calculate how far she jogs per day over the periods of time shown below. Copy and complete the table. Show your working.

Period of time	1 day	1 week	1 fortnight	Month of May	6-week summer holidays
Total distance run (km)	14	182	392	1178	2016
Distance run per day (km)					

2. Rearrange each set of 6 digits in the vertices of the hexagon to make a ThHTO ÷ TO division calculation that equals the number in the circle.

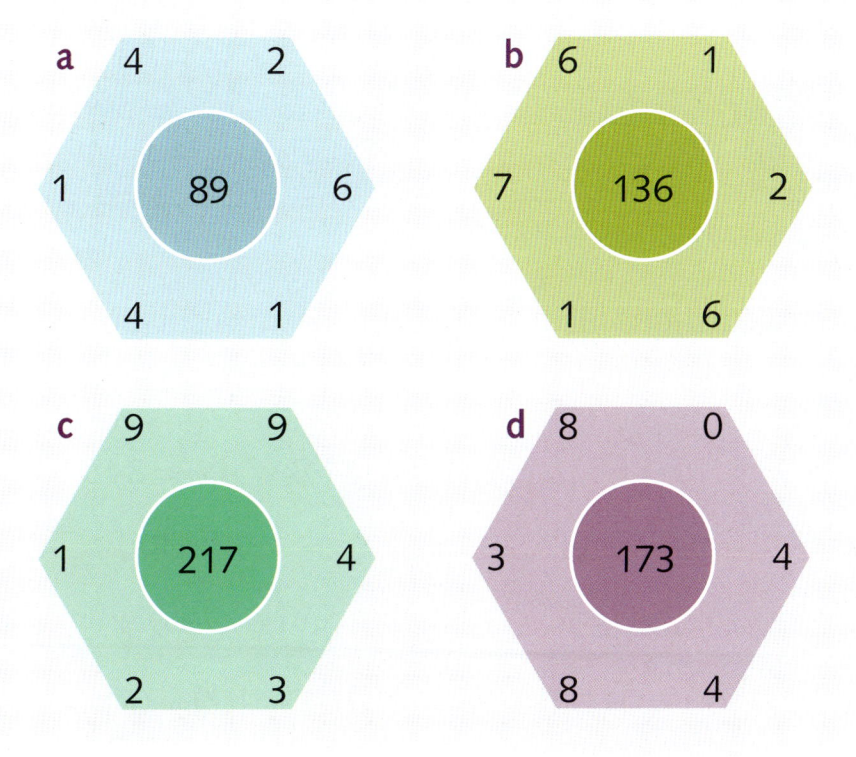

a) 4, 2, 1, 6, 4, 1 — circle: 89

b) 6, 1, 7, 2, 1, 6 — circle: 136

c) 9, 9, 1, 4, 2, 3 — circle: 217

d) 8, 0, 3, 4, 8, 4 — circle: 173

Hint
- The four digits at the top of the hexagon are the digits that make up the 4-digit number.
- The two digits at the bottom of the hexagon are the digits that make up the 2-digit number.

Unit 8, Week 2, Lesson 1

Dividing decimals using mental methods and the formal written method

- Use mental methods to divide a decimal by a 1-digit number
- Use the formal written method of short division to divide a decimal by a 1-digit number

Challenge 1

1 For each machine, work out the output number for each input number.

a ×10
- 0·6
- 0·15
- 4·07
- 5·4
- 0·09

b ×100
- 0·04
- 6·3
- 1·08
- 0·17
- 4·92

c ÷10
- 9
- 3·8
- 7·7
- 62·4
- 0·2

d ÷100
- 59
- 8
- 72
- 4
- 12

2 Malik answered each of these calculations incorrectly. Copy each calculation and write the correct answer.

a 0·3 × 10 = 30 ✗   b 5·08 × 10 = 58 ✗   c 34·8 × 100 = 348 ✗

d 18 ÷ 100 = 1·8 ✗   e 43·7 ÷ 10 = 0·437 ✗   f 0·08 × 10 = 8 ✗

g 4·1 ÷ 10 = 41 ✗   h 8·05 × 100 = 85 ✗   i 6 ÷ 100 = 0·6 ✗

j 13 ÷ 10 = 0·13 ✗   k 34 ÷ 100 = 0·034 ✗   l 0·01 × 100 = 0·1 ✗

Challenge 2

1. Sort the calculations into two groups: those you can work out using mental methods and those where you need to use a written method.

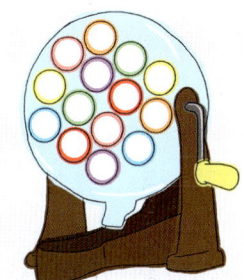

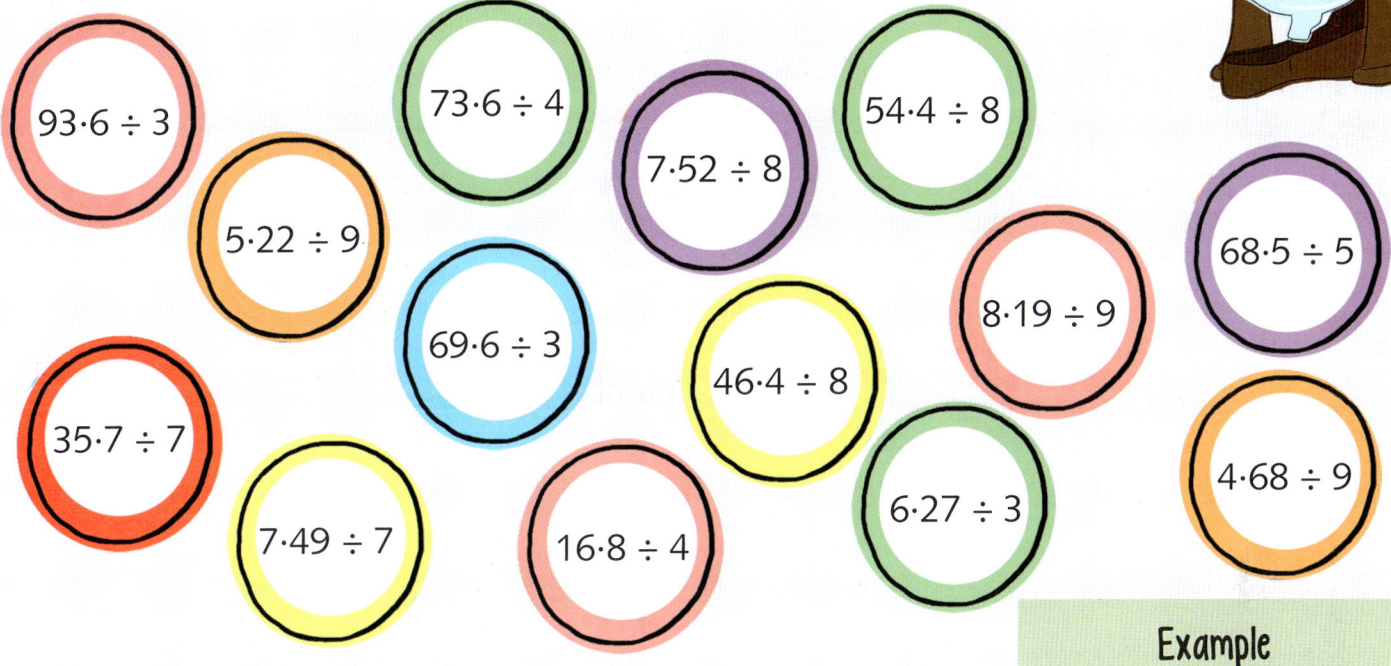

- 93·6 ÷ 3
- 73·6 ÷ 4
- 54·4 ÷ 8
- 5·22 ÷ 9
- 7·52 ÷ 8
- 68·5 ÷ 5
- 69·6 ÷ 3
- 8·19 ÷ 9
- 35·7 ÷ 7
- 46·4 ÷ 8
- 4·68 ÷ 9
- 7·49 ÷ 7
- 16·8 ÷ 4
- 6·27 ÷ 3

2. Work out the answer to each calculation in Question 1. For the calculations that need a written method, use the formal written method of short division. Remember to estimate the answer first.

Example

27·6 ÷ 6 → 30 ÷ 6 = 5

```
   T O · t h
       4 · 6
6 | 2 7 · ³6
```

You will need:
- 0–9 or 1–10 dice

Challenge 3

Play this game with a partner. Take turns to:

- Choose a number from below and write it down (you can only choose each number once).
- Roll the dice.
- Divide your chosen number by the number on the dice. Choose the most appropriate method to calculate the answer: mental or written.
- Write the calculation and the answer to 2 decimal places. Show any working out.

The person with the smallest answer scores one point. The first person to score five points is the winner.

35·6   66·6   62·4   94·5   24·8   49·2   73·5   16·8   53·4   13·4

Unit 8, Week 2, Lesson 2

Dividing decimals using the expanded written method of long division

- Use the expanded written method of long division to divide a decimal by a 2-digit number
- Estimate and check the answer to a calculation

Challenge 1

Find the missing numbers.

a 5·6 × 🍁 = 560
b 3·32 × 🍁 = 332
c 8·7 × 🍁 = 87
d 4·9 × 🍁 = 49
e 6·78 × 🍁 = 678
f 0·47 × 🍁 = 47
g 56·2 × 🍁 = 562
h 0·39 × 🍁 = 39
i 7·59 × 100 = 🍁
j 🍁 × 100 = 345
k 0·03 × 100 = 🍁
l 🍁 × 10 = 21
m 0·19 × 🍁 = 19
n 🍁 × 100 = 46
o 1·11 × 🍁 = 111

Challenge 2

1 For each division calculation write your estimate, then use the expanded written method to work out the answer. Choose your method from the examples given.

Example
58·32 ÷ 18

58·32 ÷ 18 is equivalent to 5832 ÷ 18 ÷ 100

```
        3 2 4
    ┌─────────
18  │ 5 8 3 2
    − 5 4 0 0   (300 × 18)
    ─────────
        4 3 2
    −   3 6 0   (20 × 18)
    ─────────
          7 2
    −     7 2   (4 × 18)
    ─────────
            0
```

324 ÷ 100 = 3·24

```
        3 · 2 4
    ┌─────────
18  │ 5 8 · 3 2
    − 5 4 · 0 0   (300 × 18)
    ─────────
        4 · 3 2
    −   3 · 6 0   (20 × 18)
    ─────────
        0 · 7 2
    −   0 · 7 2   (4 × 18)
    ─────────
        0 · 0 0
```

a 25·2 ÷ 18

b 93·6 ÷ 13

c 68·40 ÷ 15

d 58·86 ÷ 18

e 27·56 ÷ 13

f 68·4 ÷ 19

g 79·42 ÷ 19

h 89·6 ÷ 35

i 15·84 ÷ 33

2 Using each digit only once, make each of the following statements true.

a 0 1 2 3 8   ☐☐·☐ ÷ ☐☐ = 1·6

b 0 1 3 6 8   ☐☐·☐ ÷ ☐☐ = 1·7

c 1 3 4 6 8   ☐☐·☐ ÷ ☐☐ = 2·4

d 1 2 3 4 5   ☐☐·☐ ÷ ☐☐ = 3·8

Hint Each of the 2-digit numbers is a 'teen' number.

Challenge 3

1 Find the answer to each of these problems.

a 14 friends go to a cafe to celebrate a birthday. The bill comes to a total of €93.52. They share the cost equally between them. How much do they each pay?

b Jasper practises after school for the long jump competition. Each time he practises he jumps 15 times. In one afternoon he jumps a total distance of 78·75 m. What is the average length of each of his jumps?

c Miriam buys 15 m of fabric costing €26.50 per metre and 23 m of another fabric costing €16.25 per metre. Both fabrics are on sale at a 15% discount. How much does she pay in total?

d Marek buys 31 cupcakes to share with his friends. His bill is €74.40 and then he gets 10% off. How much does each cupcake cost him?

2 Write three different situations when you would divide numbers including decimals.

Unit 8, Week 2, Lesson 3

Dividing decimals using the formal written method of long division

- Use the formal written method of long division to divide a decimal by a 2-digit number
- Estimate and check the answer to a calculation

Challenge 1

Copy and complete the table by dividing each number by 10 and 100.

	5	16	32	85	762	20	11	465	3267
÷ 10	0·5								
÷ 100	0·05								

Challenge 2

1 For each division calculation write your estimate, then use the formal written method to work out the answer. Choose your method from the examples shown. Where necessary, round your answers to 2 decimal places.

Example

58·32 ÷ 18

58·32 ÷ 18 is equivalent to 5832 ÷ 18 ÷ 100

```
      3 2 4
18 | 5 8 3 2
   - 5 4 ↓
       4 3
     - 3 6 ↓
         7 2
       - 7 2
           0
```

```
      3 · 2 4
18 | 5 8 · 3 2
   - 5 4 · ↓
       4 · 3
     - 3 · 6 ↓
         0 · 7 2
       - 0 · 7 2
               0
```

324 ÷ 100 = 3·24

a 61·2 ÷ 18
b 41·6 ÷ 13
c 68·79 ÷ 13
d 18·76 ÷ 22
e 91·28 ÷ 14
f 53·43 ÷ 13
g 73·22 ÷ 21
h 52·08 ÷ 14

2. Four shops sell packets of Ginger Snaps. Work out the price that each shop charges for 1 packet of Ginger Snaps.

Bargain Biscuits
15 packets of Ginger Snaps for €54.60

The Ginger Shop
18 packets of Ginger Snaps for €51.66

Cheap Sweets
12 packets of Ginger snaps for €30.24

Everything For Tea
13 packets of Ginger Snaps for €40.04

Challenge 3

1. Timothy sells products round the country. He drives to see each of his clients. Calculate the length of his journey, the speed he travels at, and how long it takes him on average to reach his destination.
Copy and complete the table.
Show your working.

Distance travelled (kilometres)	192·5	583		175	246
Speed travelled (kilometres/h)	55	65	46		
Time taken (h)			19	25	6

2. Write three of your own word problems using the information in the table above. Give them to a friend to solve. Check if their answers to the word problems match your answers in the table.

Unit 8, Week 2, Lesson 4

Solving word problems (3)

- Solve word problems rounding answers to a suitable degree of accuracy where necessary
- Estimate and check the answer to a calculation

Challenge 1

Follow the instructions to find the final number.

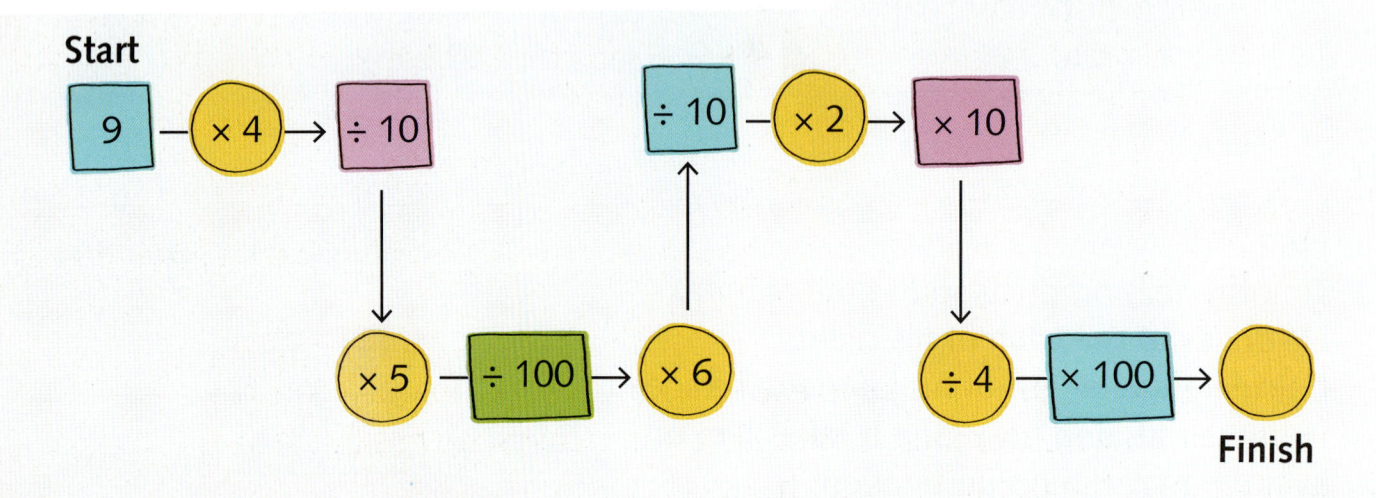

Start: 9 → ×4 → ÷10 → ×5 → ÷100 → ×6 → ÷10 → ×2 → ×10 → ÷4 → ×100 → Finish

Challenge 2

Find the answer to each of these questions about a sewing and fabric shop, rounding your answer appropriately if necessary. Remember to use estimation to check your answers.

a. Jagdish buys 65·1 m of fabric. He cuts it into 3 even pieces. What is the length of each piece? If a suit can be made from 4 m of fabric, how many suits can be made from each piece?

b. If elastic costs €3.56 per metre, how much does it cost for 60 cm of elastic?

c. The sewing and fabric shop sells different coloured ribbons in metre lengths. Laura pays €64.32 for 12 metres of purple ribbon. How much does the ribbon cost per metre?

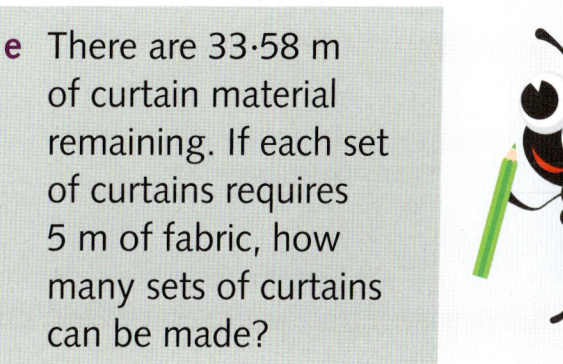

d Zips cost €9.65 per tub. Ben buys 6 tubs. He takes a €50 note out of his wallet. How much more money does he need?

e There are 33·58 m of curtain material remaining. If each set of curtains requires 5 m of fabric, how many sets of curtains can be made?

f Kara buys a sewing machine for €87.40. She receives a 25% discount in the sale. How much does she pay for her sewing machine?

g Which costs more per button: a tub of 24 buttons at 26c each or a tub of 18 buttons for €6.48?

h Conran buys 22 boxes of sequins. He pays €18.70 in total. How much does 1 box of sequins cost?

2 Look carefully at the answers to each of the questions in Question 1. Work out how much money the sewing and fabric shop has taken in total from all the customers who have made a purchase.

Challenge 3

1 Write an explanation for each of the following.

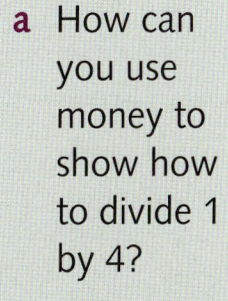

a How can you use money to show how to divide 1 by 4?

b Why does finding the cost of items usually include multiplying and dividing of whole numbers and decimals?

c Explain how 5·2 × 1·7 is similar to the calculation 52 × 17.

d Explain how multiplying and dividing decimals is similar to calculating with whole numbers.

2 Make up a word problem to match the calculation 10·98 ÷ 3.

Unit 8, Week 3, Lesson 1

Perimeter and area

Know that shapes with the same perimeters can have different areas and vice versa

Challenge 1

Each small square is 1 cm across. For each shape find:
- the perimeter in centimetres (cm)
- the area in square centimetres (cm^2)

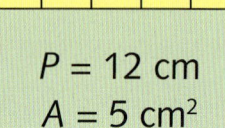

Example

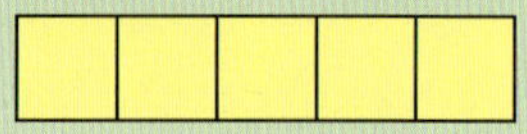

$P = 12$ cm
$A = 5$ cm^2

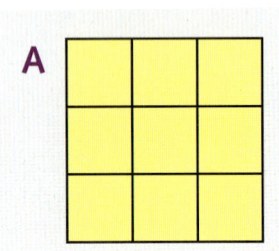

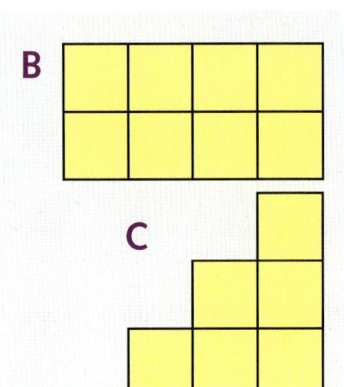

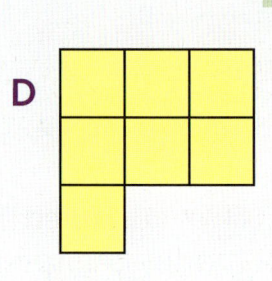

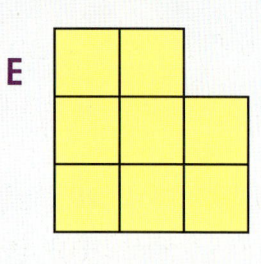

A B C D E

Challenge 2

1 Each small square is 1 cm across. Find the area and perimeter of each of the blue shaded shapes.

Example

$A = 12$ cm^2
$P = 20$ cm

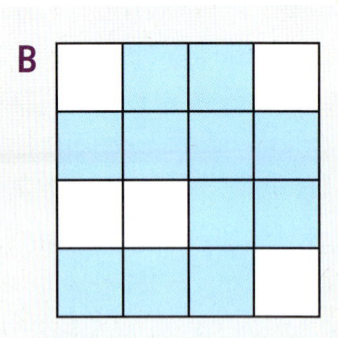

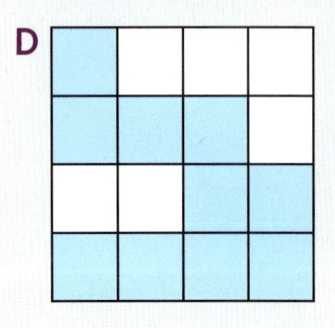

A B C D

92

2. Using Resource 57: Equal perimeters, draw six shapes that have a perimeter of 20 cm and find the area of each one.

You will need:
- Resource 57: Equal perimeters
- ruler

3. Peter bought 24 square slabs measuring 1 metre by 1 metre to tile his patio. Find the perimeter and area of his patio for each rectangle of 24 slabs.

   a 12 m long by 2 m wide   b 8 m long by 3 m wide   c 6 m long by 4 m wide

4. A landscape gardener ordered 60 square slabs measuring 1 metre by 1 metre. List the different rectangular arrangements he can make. Then write the perimeter and area of each rectangle.

Challenge 3

1. A farmer has 40 metres of fencing to make a rectangular enclosure in his barn for his sheep and lambs.

   a List all the possible measurements for his rectangular enclosure in whole metres.

   b Which measurements will give the largest area for the sheep and lambs?

Example
16 m × 4 m
P = 40 m
A = 64 m²

2. The farmer considers using one wall of the barn for one side of the enclosure and 40 metres of fencing for the other three sides. What is the largest rectangular area he can enclose with his fencing?

Key
barn wall
fencing - - - - - -

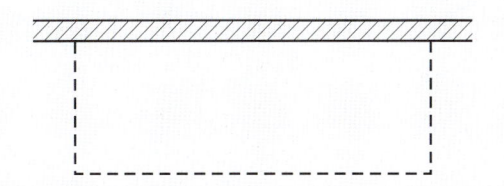

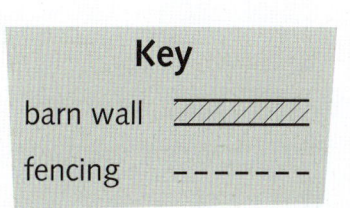

3. His son suggests that he could use two walls of the barn that are at right angles for two sides of the enclosure and use the 40 metres of fencing for the other two sides. What is the largest rectangular area he can enclose with his fencing?

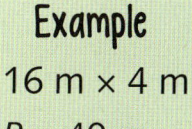

93

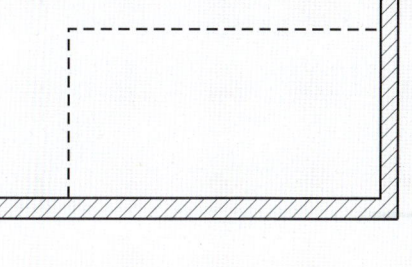

Unit 8, Week 3, Lesson 2

Surface area

Know when to use the formula for the area of shapes

Challenge 1

Find the surface area of each cuboid by counting the squares.

A

B

Example

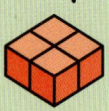

Visible 1 cm squares: 8

Hidden 1 cm squares: 8

Surface area = 16 cm^2

Challenge 2

1. Each net of a 3-D shape is drawn on 1 cm squared paper. Calculate the surface area of each net in square centimetres.

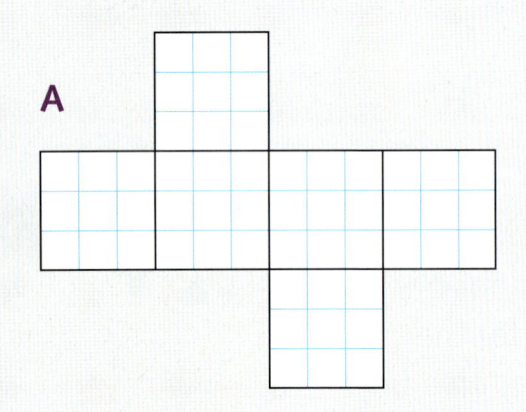

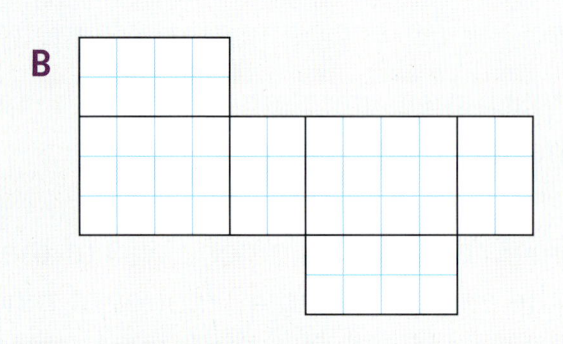

   A

   B

2. Calculate the surface area of each cuboid and record your answers in a table. Look for a pattern in your results and use the pattern to work out the surface area of the next two cuboids, F and G, in the sequence.

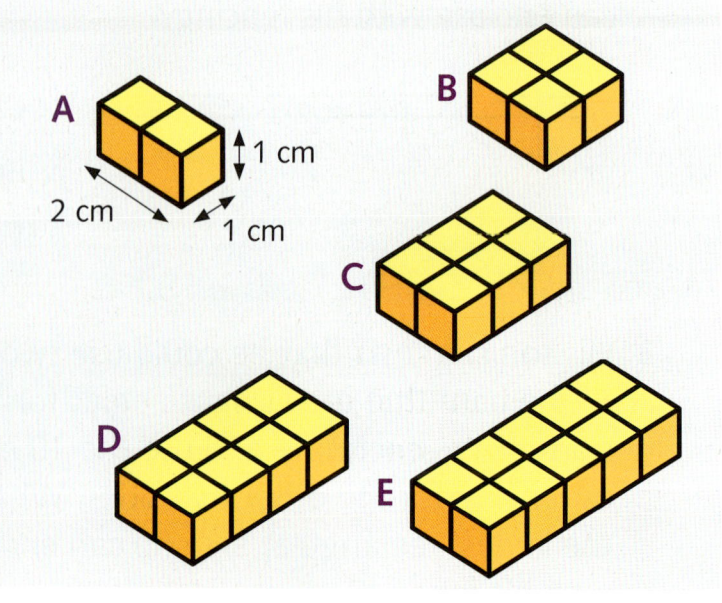

   A — 2 cm, 1 cm, 1 cm

   B

   C

   D

   E

94

3 Each cube is built using 1 cm³ cubes. Copy and complete the table below.

You will need:
- ruler

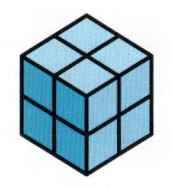

Length of one side (cm)	1	2	3	4
Surface area of one face (cm²)	1			
Surface area of the cube (cm²)	6			

4 Using your table from Question 3, find the surface area of cubes with sides of:

   a 5 cm   **b** 8 cm   **c** 10 cm

5 Calculate the surface area of each box below. The boxes are not drawn to scale.

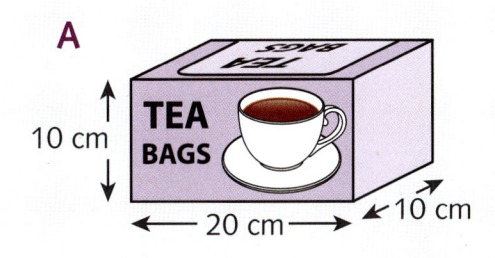

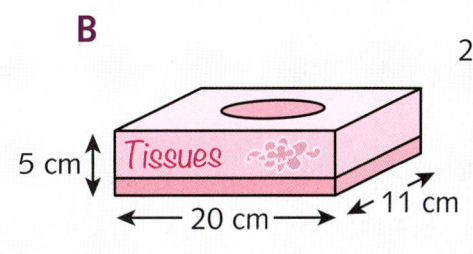

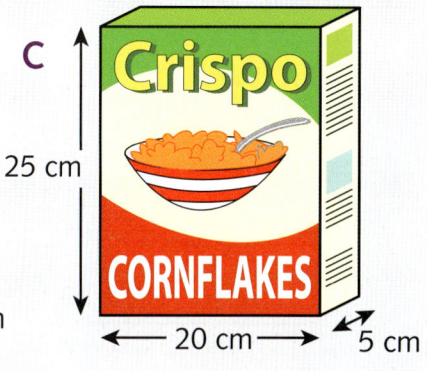

A — TEA BAGS: 10 cm, 20 cm, 10 cm

B — Tissues: 5 cm, 20 cm, 11 cm

C — Crispo CORNFLAKES: 25 cm, 20 cm, 5 cm

Challenge 3

These cubes are made using alternate red and yellow 1 cm³ cubes. For each cube, work out the total surface area that is red and the total surface area that is yellow.

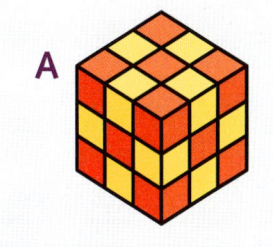

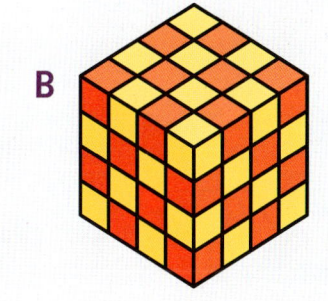

A   B

Unit 8, Week 3, Lesson 3

Area of triangles

Calculate the area of a triangle using the rule $A = \frac{1}{2}bh$

Challenge 1

1 Find the area of each blue triangle. Each small square is 1 cm across.

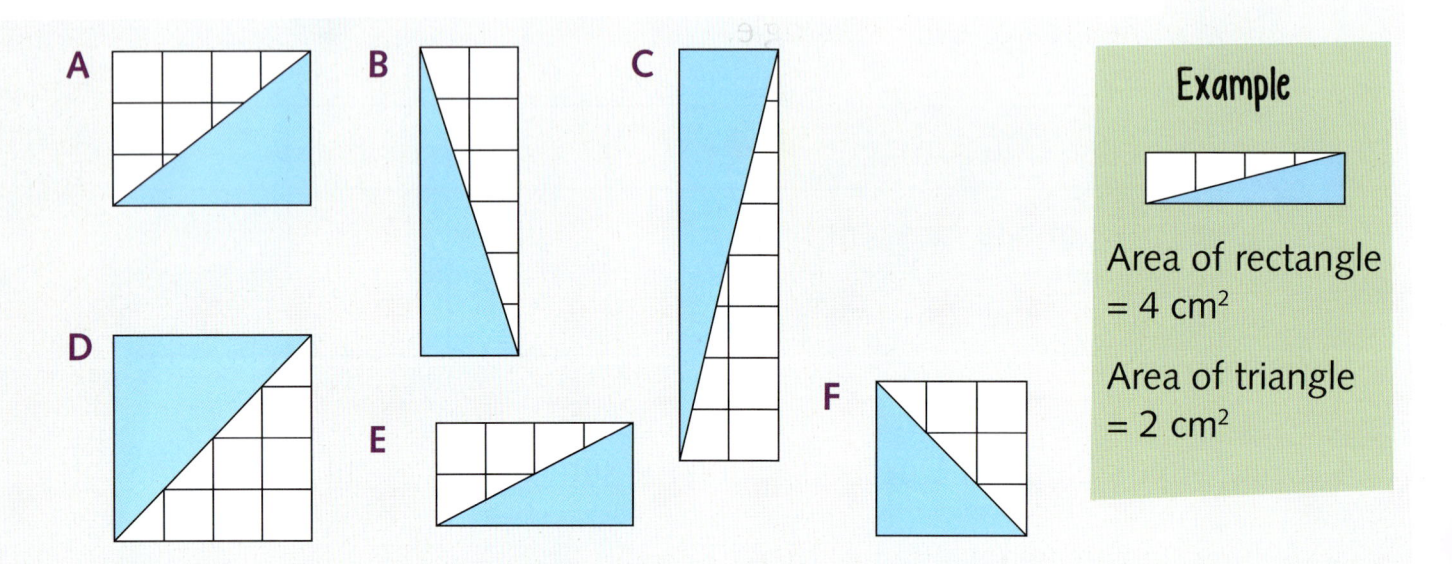

Example

Area of rectangle = 4 cm²

Area of triangle = 2 cm²

2 Write the letter of the triangle that has the same area as triangle D.

Challenge 2

1 Calculate the area of each purple triangle using the rule $A = \frac{1}{2}bh$.

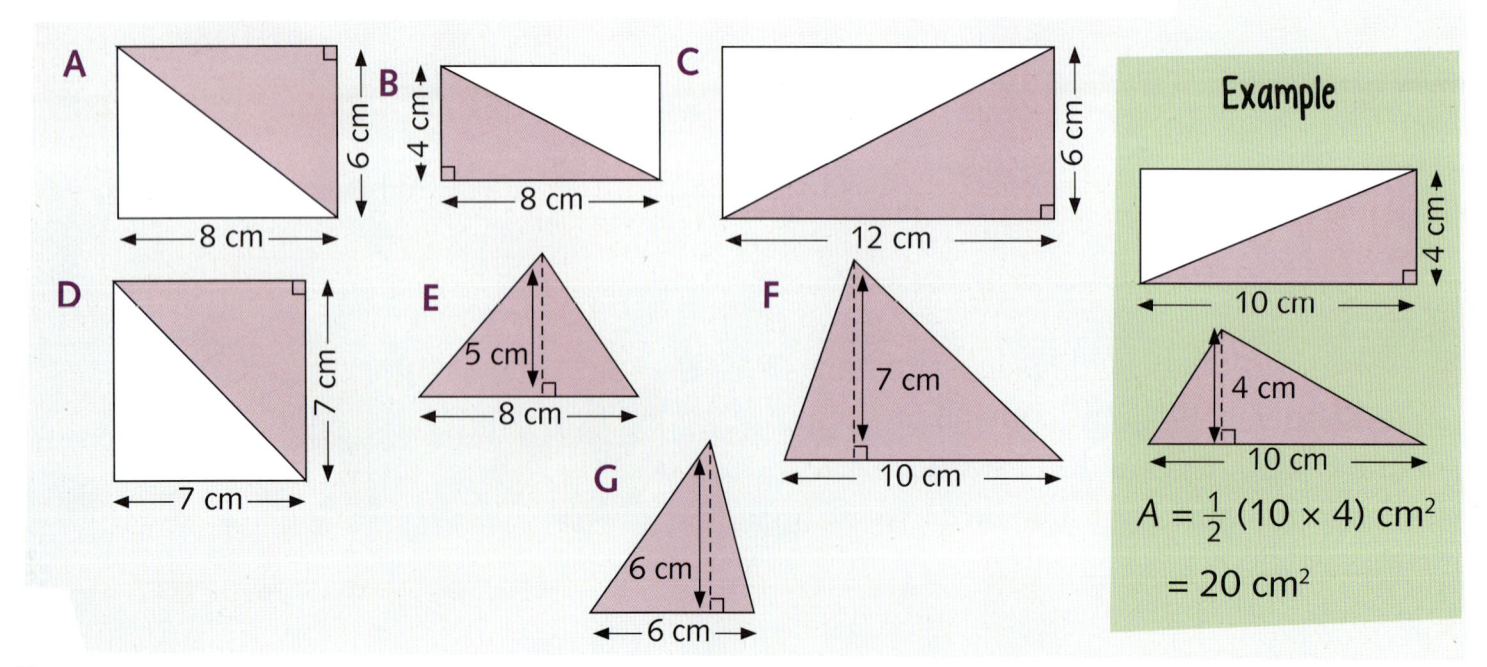

Example

$A = \frac{1}{2}(10 \times 4)$ cm²

= 20 cm²

2 Turn triangles into rectangles.

- Copy each yellow triangle onto 1 cm squared paper and cut it out.
- Make one cut at the midpoint of the longest side. Transform your triangle into a rectangle.
- Glue each rectangle in your exercise book or on a piece of paper.
- Write the area of each rectangle.

You will need:
- 1 cm squared paper
- ruler
- scissors
- glue

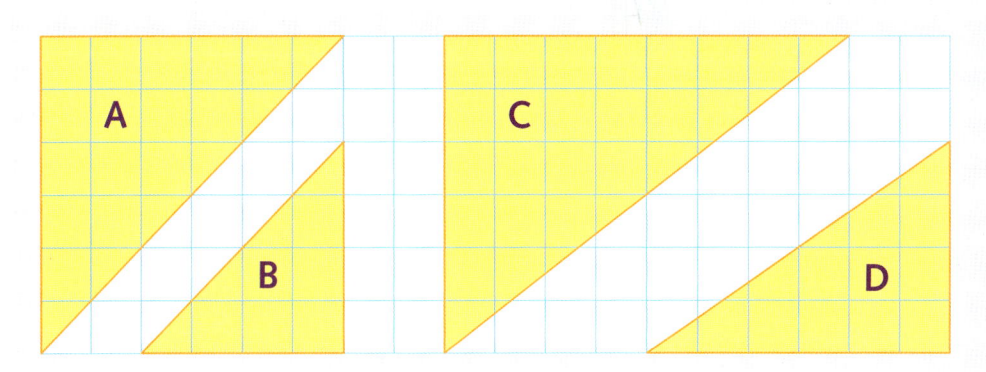

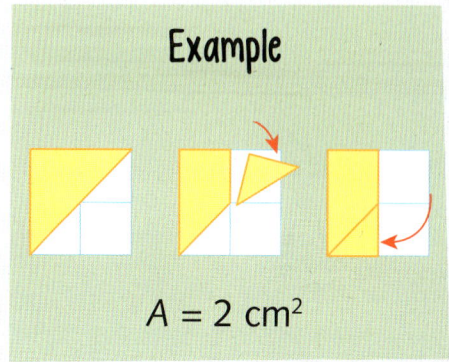

Example

$A = 2$ cm^2

Challenge 3

You can find the area of the red triangle by subtracting the area of the pieces outside the triangle from the area of the square. Calculate the area of these red triangles in cm^2. Show the steps in your working. The dots are 1 cm apart.

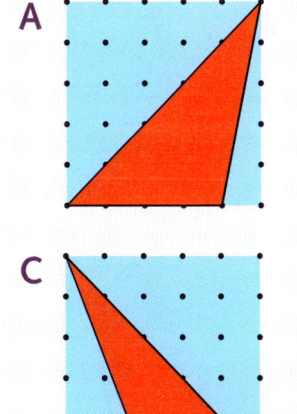

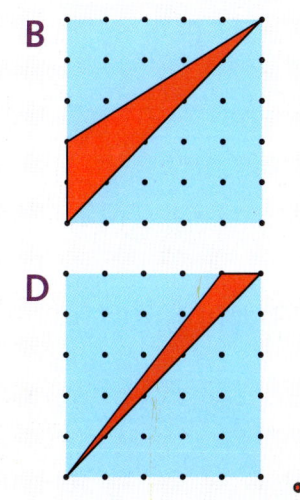

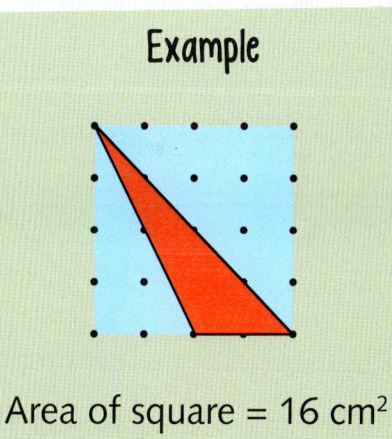

Example

Area of square = 16 cm^2

Area of pieces outside the red triangle
$= 8$ cm$^2 + 4$ cm^2
$= 12$ cm^2

Area of red triangle = 4 cm^2

Unit 8, Week 3, Lesson 4

Area of parallelograms

Calculate the area of a parallelogram using the rule $A = bh$ and relate the dissection of a rectangle to the area of a parallelogram

Rule

Finding the area of parallelograms:

- Cut a right-angled triangle from one end of the parallelogram.
- Slide the triangle to the other side of the parallelogram to make a rectangle.

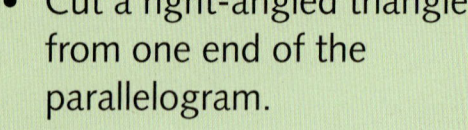

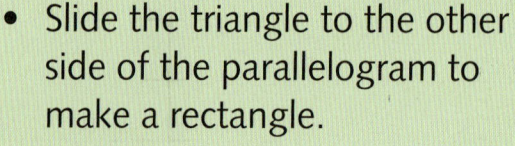

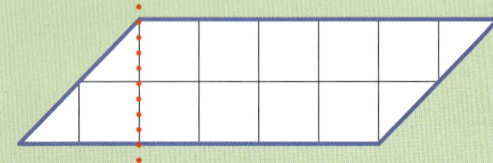

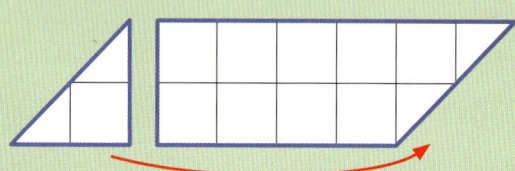

- The parallelogram now has the same base and height as the rectangle. So you can use the rule $A = bh$.

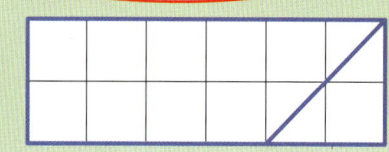

$A = bh$
$= (6 \times 2)$ cm^2
$= 12$ cm^2

Challenge 1

Find the area of each parallelogram in cm^2. Each grid square is 1 cm across.

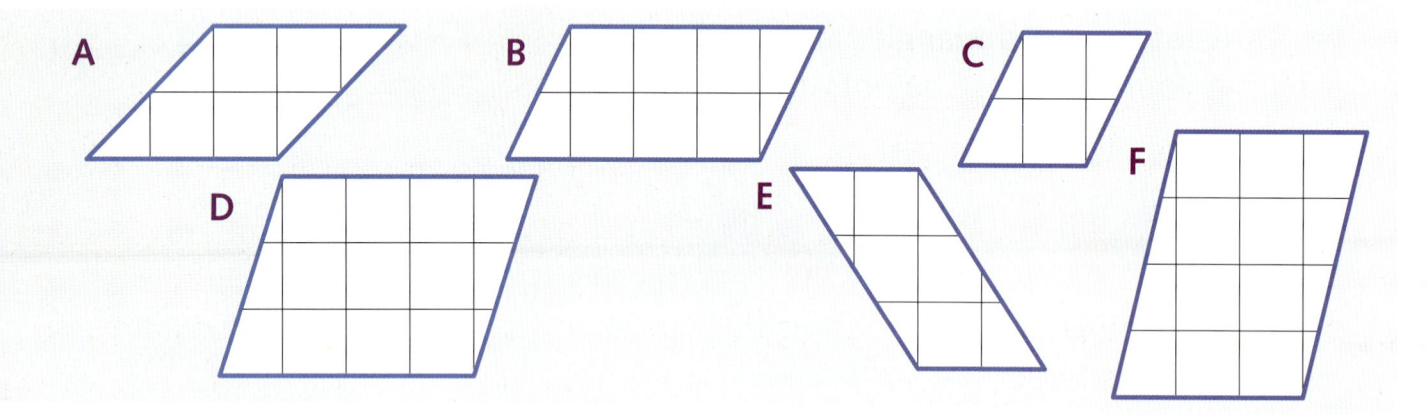

A B C D E F

Challenge 2

1 Calculate the area of each parallelogram using the rule $A = bh$.

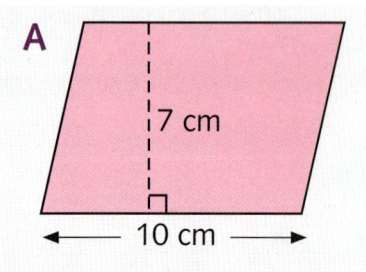

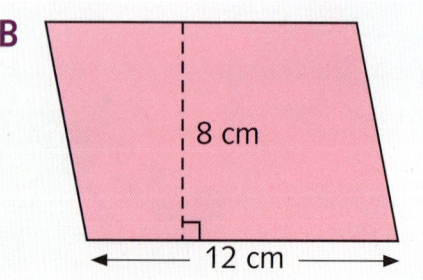

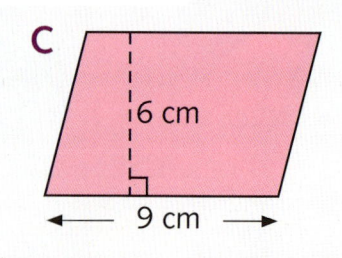

A: 7 cm, 10 cm
B: 8 cm, 12 cm
C: 6 cm, 9 cm

98

2 Copy shapes A to D onto 1 cm square dot paper.

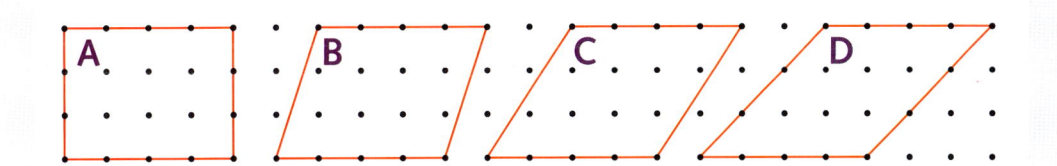

You will need:
- 1 cm squared dot paper
- ruler

a Draw and letter the next two parallelograms in the sequence.

b Copy and complete the table for the area of each shape.

Shape	A	B	C	D	E	F
Area (cm²)						

3 Copy the shapes P, Q and R onto 1 cm square dot paper.

a Draw and letter the next three parallelograms in the sequence.

b Copy and complete the table below for the area of each shape.

c Explain the pattern.

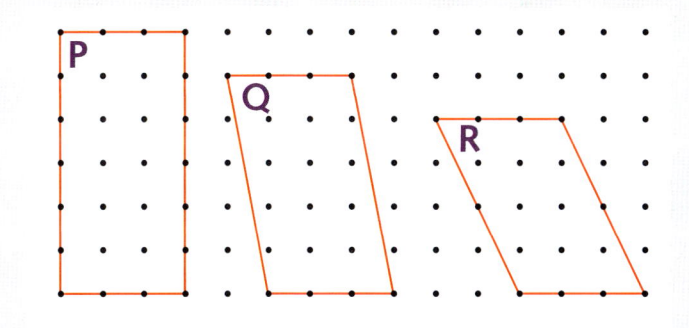

Shape	P	Q	R	S	T	U
Area (cm²)						

Challenge 3

Use what you know about finding the area of a parallelogram to find the area of each isosceles trapezium.

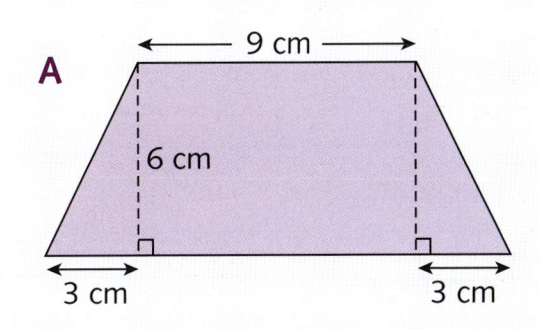

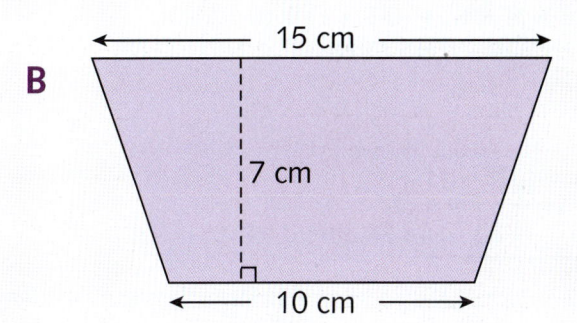

A: 9 cm (top), 6 cm (height), 3 cm and 3 cm (bottom extensions)

B: 15 cm (top), 7 cm (height), 10 cm (bottom)

Maths facts

Addition and subtraction

Whole numbers

Example: 456 287 + 359 849

```
  456 287
+ 359 849
---------
  816 136
  1 1 1 1
```

Example: 746 291 − 298 354

```
   6 13 15 12 8 11
   7̶4̶6̶ 2̶9̶1̶
 − 298 354
 ---------
   447 937
```

Decimals

Example: 57·486 + 45·378

```
   57·486
 + 45·378
 --------
  102·864
    1  11
```

Example: 63·237 − 45·869

```
   5 12  11 12 17
   6̶3̶ · 2̶3̶7̶
 − 45·869
 --------
   17·368
```

Multiplication and division

Written methods – short multiplication

Whole numbers

Example: 5643 × 8

Formal written method

```
    5643
 ×  5 3 2 8
 -------
   45144
```

Decimals

Example: 4·83 × 6

Partitioning

4·83 × 6 = (4 × 6) + (0·8 × 6) + (0·03 × 6)
         = 24 + 4·8 + 0·18
         = 28·98

Grid method

×	4	0·8	0·03
6	24	4·8	0·18	= 28·98

Expanded written method

4·83 × 6 is equivalent to 483 × 6 ÷ 100

```
    483
 ×    6
 -----
     18  ( 3 × 6)
    480  ( 80 × 6)
   2400  (400 × 6)
 -----
   2898
```

2898 ÷ 100 = 28·98

Formal written method

```
    483
 ×  4 1 6
 -----
   2898
```

2898 ÷ 100 = 28·98

100

Written methods – long multiplication
Whole numbers

Example: 285 × 63

Partitioning

285 × 63 = (200 × 63) + (80 × 63) + (5 × 63)
          = 12 600 + 5040 + 315
          = 17 955

Grid method

×	200	80	5
60	12 000	4800	300
3	600	240	15

  17 100
+   855
  17 955

Expanded written method

```
    285                    285
  ×  63                  ×  63
 17 300  (285 × 60)        855  (285 × 3)
    855  (285 ×  3)     17 300  (285 × 60)
  17955                  17955
```
or

Formal written method

```
    285
  ×  63
    855
  17 300
  17955
```

Decimals

Example: 7·56 × 34

Partitioning

7·56 × 34 = (7 × 34) + (0·5 × 34) + (0·06 × 34)
           = 238 + 17 + 2·04
           = 257·04

Grid method

×	7	0·5	0·06
30	210	15	1·8
4	28	2	0·24

  226·80
+ 30·24
  257·04

Expanded written method

7·56 × 34 is equivalent to 756 × 34 ÷ 100

```
    756                      756
  ×  34                    ×  34
  22 680  (756 × 30)        3024  (756 × 4)
   3024   (756 ×  4)      22 680  (756 × 30)
  25704                   25704
     1                       1
```
or

25 704 ÷ 100 = 257·04   25 704 ÷ 100 = 257·04

Formal written method

7·56 × 34 is equivalent to 756 × 34 ÷ 100

```
    756
  ×  34
   3024
  22 680
  25704
     1
```

25 704 ÷ 100 = 257·04

Written methods – short division
Whole numbers

Example: 1838 ÷ 8

Whole number remainder

```
      2 2 9 r 6
  8 ) 1 8 ²3 ⁷8
```

Fraction remainder

```
      2 2 9 ¾
  8 ) 1 8 ²3 ⁷8
```

Decimal remainder

```
      2 2 9 · 7 5
  8 ) 1 8 ²3 ⁷8 · ⁶0 ⁴0
```

101

Decimals

Example: 45·36 ÷ 6

45·36 ÷ 6 is equivalent to 4536 ÷ 6 ÷ 100

```
       7 · 5 6                        7 5 6
   6 ) 4 5 ·³3 ³6        or       6 ) 4 5³3 ³6
```

756 ÷ 100 = 7·56

Written methods – long division

Whole numbers

Example: 5836 ÷ 18

Expanded written method

```
            3 2 4  r 4
     18 ) 5 8 3 6
        - 5 4 0 0      (300 × 18)
          ³ ¹³
            4 3 6
        -   3 6 0      ( 20 × 18)
              7 6
        -     7 2      (  4 × 18)
                4
```

5836 ÷ 18 = 324 r 4   or $324\frac{2}{9}$

Formal written method

```
            3 2 4  r 4
     18 ) 5 8 3 6
        - 5 4 ↓
            4 3
        -   3 6 ↓
              7 6
        -     7 2
                4
```

5836 ÷ 18 = 324 r 4   or $324\frac{2}{9}$

Decimals

Example: 58·32 ÷ 18

Expanded written method

58·32 ÷ 18 is equivalent to 5832 ÷ 18 ÷ 100

```
            3 2 4                                     3 · 2 4
     18 ) 5 8 3 2                              18 ) 5 8 · 3 2
        - 5 4 0 0   (300 × 18)      or            - 5 4 · 0 0   ( 3 × 18)
          ³ ¹³                                      ³ ¹³
            4 3 2                                     4 · 3 2
        -   3 6 0   ( 20 × 18)                    -  3 · 6 0   ( 0·2 × 18)
              7 2                                     0 · 7 2
        -     7 2   (  4 × 18)                    -  0 · 7 2   (0·04 × 18)
                0                                     0 · 0 0
```

324 ÷ 100 = 3·24

Formal written method

58·32 ÷ 18 is equivalent to 5832 ÷ 18 ÷ 100

```
       3 2 4
18 ) 5 8 3 2
   - 5 4 ↓
       4 3
   -   3 6 ↓
           7 2
       -   7 2
               0
```

or

```
       3 · 2 4
18 ) 5 8 · 3 2
   - 5 4 · ↓
       4 · 3
   -   3 · 6 ↓
           0 · 7 2
       -   0 · 7 2
                   0
```

324 ÷ 100 = 3·24

Fractions, decimals and percentages

$\frac{1}{100} = 0.01 = 1\%$ $\frac{2}{100} = \frac{1}{50} = 0.02 = 2\%$ $\frac{4}{100} = \frac{1}{25} = 0.04 = 4\%$

$\frac{5}{100} = \frac{1}{20} = 0.05 = 5\%$ $\frac{10}{100} = \frac{1}{10} = 0.1 = 10\%$ $\frac{20}{100} = \frac{1}{5} = 0.2 = 20\%$

$\frac{25}{100} = \frac{1}{4} = 0.25 = 25\%$ $\frac{40}{100} = \frac{2}{5} = 0.4 = 40\%$ $\frac{50}{100} = \frac{1}{2} = 0.5 = 50\%$

$\frac{75}{100} = \frac{3}{4} = 0.75 = 75\%$ $\frac{80}{100} = \frac{4}{5} = 0.8 = 80\%$ $\frac{100}{100} = \frac{10}{10} = 1 = 100\%$

$\frac{2}{5} + \frac{4}{5} = \frac{6}{5}$
$= 1\frac{1}{5}$

$\frac{7}{8} - \frac{3}{8} = \frac{4}{8}$
$= \frac{1}{2}$

$\frac{2}{3} \times 4 = \frac{2}{3} \times \frac{4}{1}$
$= \frac{2 \times 4}{3 \times 1}$
$= \frac{8}{3}$
$= 2\frac{2}{3}$

$2\frac{3}{4} \times 3 = \frac{11}{4} \times 3$
$= \frac{11 \times 3}{4 \times 1}$
$= \frac{33}{4}$
$= 8\frac{1}{4}$

$9\frac{2}{3} + 6\frac{4}{5}$
$9 + 6 = 15$
$\frac{2}{3} + \frac{4}{5} = \frac{10}{15} + \frac{12}{15}$
$= \frac{22}{15}$
$= 1\frac{7}{15}$
$1\frac{7}{15} + 15 = 16\frac{7}{15}$

$11\frac{3}{4} - 7\frac{2}{6}$
$11 - 7 = 4$
$\frac{3}{4} - \frac{2}{6} = \frac{9}{12} - \frac{4}{12}$
$= \frac{5}{12}$
$\frac{5}{12} + 4 = 4\frac{5}{12}$

$\frac{1}{2} \times \frac{3}{4} = \frac{1 \times 3}{2 \times 4}$
$= \frac{3}{8}$

$\frac{2}{3} \div 4 = \frac{2}{3 \times 4}$
$= \frac{2}{12}$
$= \frac{1}{6}$

Measurement

Length

1 km = 1000 m = 100 000 cm
0·1 km = 100 m = 10 000 cm = 100 000 mm
0·01 km = 10 m = 1000 cm = 10 000 mm
1 m = 100 cm = 1000 mm
0·1 m = 10 cm = 100 mm

0·01 m = 1 cm = 10 mm
0·001 m = 0·1 cm = 1 mm
1 cm = 10 mm
0·1 cm = 1 mm

Metric units and imperial units – Length

1 km ≈ $\frac{5}{8}$ miles (8 km ≈ 5 miles)
1 inch ≈ 2·5 cm

Capacity

1 litre = 1000 ml
0·1 l = 100 ml
0·01 l = 10 ml
0·001 l = 1 ml
1 cl = 10 ml

24-hour time

Perimeter, area and volume

P = perimeter   A = area   V = volume
l = length   w = width   b = base   h = height

Perimeter of a rectangle
P = 2(l + w)

Perimeter of a square
P = 4 × l or   P = 4l

Area of a rectangle
A = l × w   or   A = lw

Area of a triangle
A = $\frac{1}{2}$ × b × h   or   A = $\frac{1}{2}$bh

Area of a parallelogram
A = b × h   or   A = bh

Volume of a cuboid
V = l × w × h   or   V = $l$wh

Mass

1 t = 1000 kg   1 kg = 1000 g   0·1 kg = 100g   0·01 kg = 10 g   0·001 kg = 1 g

Geometry

Parts of a circle

circumference
centre
radius
diameter

Coordinates

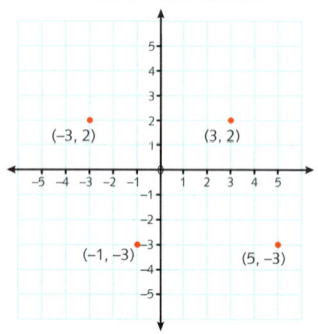

(−3, 2)   (3, 2)
(−1, −3)   (5, −3)

Translation

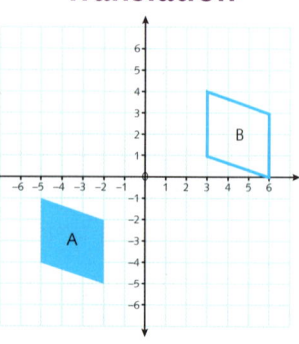

Shape A has been translated 8 squares to the right and 5 squares up.

Reflection

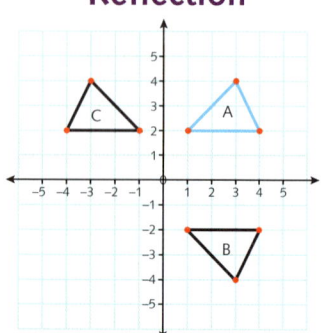

Shape A has been reflected in the x-axis (Shape B) and in the y-axis (Shape C).